12 PRINCIPLES OF
FOLLOW ME

THE DIFFERENCE BETWEEN
Believing in Jesus and Following Him

Aaron Zapata

*12 Principles of Follow Me - The Difference Between
Believing in Jesus and Following Him*

by Aaron Zapata

Printed in the United States of America

ISBN 978-1-7360745-0-3

Unless otherwise indicated, Bible quotations are taken from the New American Standard Bible.

v1.3

DEDICATION

This book is dedicated to my Lord and Savior Jesus Christ. His hand has guided my life and He has made me who I am today and He gets all the glory.

I'd also like to thank my wife, Dawn who has been my biggest supporter and cheerleader. Thank you, love for blessing me every day. Finally, I'd like to thank my sons, Levi and Malachi, whom I am blessed to call my children.

My prayer is that God will bless you and that you will be transformed more into the likeness of Christ.

"You believe that there is one God. Good! Even the demons believe that – and shudder."

James 2:19 NIV

If demons can believe in God and shudder, then simply believing in God does not equate to salvation; we must also follow.

Table of Contents

INTRODUCTION

Prov-i-dence [prov-i-du*hn*s] (noun)

*"The foreseeing care and guidance of God over
the creatures of the earth."[1]*

I firmly believe that you are reading this book because God wanted you to. It is not an accident that you decided to thumb through the pages. I don't know why you decided to pick up this little book. Maybe it was the cover or maybe it was the title that stirred something within you. You saw it, read the title, and something in your spirit stirred within you. *"I wonder what he has to say about what it means to 'Follow Me'?"* you might have asked yourself. Whatever the case may be, the fact is you picked up this book and started to read it. The most important decision you will make right now is whether or not you will continue to read it and allow the principles to transform your life.

Do you really want to know what it means to follow Jesus? If so, it is my prayer that you will prayerfully read the 12 Principles in this book and allow God to show you how you should apply them to your life.

If you don't really want to know, you may choose to stop reading, close the book and put it back where you got it from. If that is your choice, I pray that one day, your heart will be stirred and you will come looking, not for this book, but for a deeper and more satisfying relationship with Jesus: a relationship built on truth, trust, and experience.

My prayer is that you will continue reading and that God will move in your heart as He moved in my heart when I discovered these 12 principles. Once you know Christ and follow Him, life will never be the same.

"If any man is in Christ, he is a new creature,
the old is gone, behold, new things have come."

- 2 Corinthians 5:17

In the New Testament of the Bible we are introduced to Levi, a tax collector. In his day, he would have been considered a "sinner", if you will. He was hated by his own people and considered a traitor because he profited from taking money and possessions from God's people and giving them to the hideous Roman government, led by a man in Rome, who claimed to be God. Each day, Levi would sit at his tax-collecting table taking money from his fellow Jews, and even his own family. The Romans had made the job very lucrative for tax gathers. The rule was simple, collect a certain amount per person and if you collect more, you keep the difference. Of course, everyone knew this, and so they despised Levi for profiting in this way.

One day, while Levi was sitting behind his table, he suddenly noticed a large crowd coming down the street. There was a great deal of commotion and he wasn't sure what was going on. As the crowd swelled in front of his booth, one man stepped out from the crowd and said to him, "Follow Me! Tonight we are eating at your house." Immediately Levi arose from his tax-collecting table and followed the man who had called to him. (Matthew 9:9)

We don't know if Levi had known Jesus prior to this encounter, but we do know that as a result of this encounter, he became a true follower of Jesus Christ and was never the same again.

This book examines the life of Levi, whom Jesus then renamed Matthew. It will focus on 12 life-changing principles that every authentic follower of Jesus Christ should experience as they move from believing to following Him.

1

Principle of Proximity

When you become a follower of Jesus Christ, your proximity must change from where you are, to where He is.

> *"And He [Jesus] said to them, 'Follow Me, and I will make you fishers of men.' Immediately they left their nets and followed Him."*
>
> – *Matthew 3:19-20*

We are all sedentary. We don't like to move if we don't have to. We like to settle down and grow roots and establish ourselves. We buy homes because we intend to stay where we are for as long as possible. Movement, or change, is often not easy, nor is it truly welcomed.

Few things in life result in packing up our belongings and relocating. Perhaps a job opportunity or a death in the family, or a pending natural disaster will be enough to force a move. Anyone who lives in the path of a hurricane knows that when faced with a hurricane, the best thing to do is to remove their family from the danger zone and head for safety. Homes get boarded up, store shelves are emptied, and the freeways are clogged with cars as people attempt to relocate. Their goal is simple: to get out of the way of the hurricane so that their family remains safe.

I'm always surprised at the few that decide to stay and face the storm. They stay in their homes, hoping that they will make it through the storm without much harm to their homes or themselves. Some survive and sadly, some don't.

There are clearly two different mindsets and beliefs between those that leave and those that stay. Those that heed the warning signs and listen to the authorities when they call for evacuation do so for their own good and safety. In fact, you rarely hear reports of someone who was injured or killed after they moved to a safer place, following the evacuation order.

A follower, by definition, is someone who will take orders and leadership from another person or power. A follower will go where and when his leader commands him to go regardless of the outcome, or of the convenience. If the leader rises early in the morning to begin a long journey, the follower rises and departs at the same time. If the leader decides to stop, the follower stops. If the leader says, "Go over there because it's safer," the follower does as he is told and goes to the safer place.

Of course hurricanes are dangerous and so it is easier to follow someone's instructions to get to a safer place. Every hurricane wreaks destruction and should be avoided. Our lives, however, do not always predictably lead to disaster, so we don't see the necessity to be a true follower of any other person. There are few people who can truly say they can and do follow another person unconditionally. We know our own hearts and how wicked they can be, so we shield and protect ourselves from becoming a true follower of another, especially if our lives are not in danger. The truth is, because we live life in such a guarded way, we unknowingly do the same with Jesus. We hedge our bets and reserve the right to do as we believe is best. We become like those that choose to stay and face the storm.

Levi, on the other hand, as soon as he was called by Jesus to follow Him, immediately got up and left what he was doing to literally follow after Jesus. He gets up from his table and leaves. In that moment, he became a follower of Jesus Christ and it would have been impossible for him to say 'yes' to Jesus' request and then stay where he was. He had to move.

Not all who Jesus called to follow Him, however, chose to follow. In Matthew 19:21 Jesus gives the command, "come, follow Me" to a rich young ruler who chooses not to follow Him. The Greek word used for "come" is in the active, imperative tense, which indicates a command and not a suggestion. It was the responsibility of the person receiving the command to follow it immediately. Sadly, the ruler decided that his riches were more valuable and he walked away.

As a follower of Christ, there is a change in your proximity to Him. Before accepting Christ, a gap existed between you two. The distance was obvious and was created by sin. Once saved, however, you are to grow closer and closer to Him by learning to listen to His voice and by following His leadership in your life. In essence, the gap gets smaller.

We cannot say to Jesus, "Yes, I will follow you!" and then stay where we are. Jesus will always require us to take steps toward Him and His plans for us. He requires a heart that is set on following Him.

Our actions will always indicate the true intentions and the condition of our heart. Jerry Leachman, a man I respect and admire for his service to our Lord, said it this way, "You can fake caring, but you can't fake showing up." In other words, true commitment is shown in our actions. We can say we follow Jesus, but unless our actions show it, we really aren't.

When Paul writes to the Christians in Ephesus, he reminds them that they were once "far off" and were "brought near" through Jesus Christ. Christ, in His earthly death on the cross, tore down the barriers that existed between God's chosen people, the Jews, and the rest of the human race. He made it possible for the outsiders to become insiders. When we follow after Christ, we are taken from the darkness and brought into His family, where we are included in the promises for His children.

A follower of Christ undergoes this change in proximity spiritually and physically. Before following Christ, we were far from God in both ways and after choosing to follow Him we become close in both ways. Our bodies become the temple of God (1 Corinthians 6:19) and we are spiritually filled with God's Spirit. Just as a glass cannot be filled with water unless it physically touches the water, it is the same when we are filled with God's Spirit, we are touched by God Himself.

As we follow Christ, our lives begin to show evidence that we are indeed following Him. The Psalms paint a beautiful picture of this proximity change by comparing a person of faith to a tree that is firmly planted next to a stream of water.

> *"How blessed is the man who does not walk in the counsel of the wicked, nor stand in the path of sinners, nor sit in the seat of scoffers! But his delight is in the law of the LORD, and in His law he meditates day and night.* **He will be like a tree firmly planted by streams of water,** *which yields its fruit in its season and its leaf does not wither; and in whatever he does, he prospers."*
>
> *– Psalm 1:1-3 (emphasis added)*

Throughout the Bible, water is symbolic of God's Spirit and life. In this passage, notice the proximity of the tree to the water: it is *firmly* planted next to it. Being close to the water brings life, strength, courage, endurance, and many other benefits that cannot be found elsewhere.

A follower of Christ must remain in close proximity to Christ to continue to experience the benefits of the life giving waters that He gives to His own.

In this life we face spiritual battles as large as a hurricane with just as much potential for destruction. As followers we must listen to Christ as He leads us to where we need to be. He will lead us, and a true follower will stay close to Him.

2

Principle of Possessions

When you follow Christ, you have a change in possessions.

> *"Jesus said to him, 'If you wish to be complete, go and sell your possessions and give to the poor, and you will have treasure in heaven; and come, follow Me.'"*
>
> – *Matthew 19:21*

Most of us measure our worth by the possessions we own. We count our blessings by the number of digits in our paychecks, the size of our house and its zip code, the quality of the private school our children attend, and the label on our clothes. And the more we have, the better we feel about ourselves. We look at those who have more than we do and we long for what they have. The illusion is this, "The more we own the better off we will be." We believe that we'll have more opportunities in life and that we will find security and comfort in amassing tangible assets that we can rely on during tough times.

It has been this way since the beginning of the world and this belief comes straight from Satan himself. In the Garden of Eden Satan tempted Eve with "more". She was enticed by the thought that she did not know enough. She wanted more and Satan was offering it to her. Satan's promise of more knowledge was enough to tempt her into sin.

King Solomon, the richest man to ever live, had more money, wealth, and luxuries than any other man, yet his pursuit of wealth and possessions resulted in the following declaration, "I have seen all the things that are done under the sun; all of them are meaningless, a chasing after the wind" (Ecclesiastes 1:14).

So why do we still hold tightly to our possessions? Why do we try to amass fortunes? Even as followers of Christ, we seek comfort and security in our possessions.

As an authentic follower of Christ, this perspective must change.

Prior to knowing Jesus, it is understandable that one would believe their worth and security comes from the possessions he or she owns. After choosing to follow Christ, however, it should become clear that our value, worth, security, and our identity come solely from our relationship with God.

Romans 8:17 gives us this promise: "Now if we are children, then we are heirs—heirs of God and co-heirs with Christ, if indeed we share in His sufferings in order that we may also share in His glory." We are now His children and will inherit an eternity that is beyond imagination. Nothing on this earth will compare to the future that is promised to us.

As a follower of Christ, He calls us to surrender everything to Him to allow Him to use everything we own as He sees fit. Does that mean that you will have to sell your house, liquidate your savings, and give all your money away? It might.

And if He does ask you to do that, could you say "yes"?

A wealthy person once came to Christ and asked Him what he needed to do in order to have eternal life. The young man was the ideal citizen and kept all the laws and was very righteous by all human standards. Christ then asked him to sell all of his possessions and to come and follow Him.

As discussed in the previous chapter, this rich young ruler was being asked to take immediate action.

His riches, however, proved to be too great to leave behind, and the man did not surrender and did not become a true follower of Christ.

It is clear from this example that possessions are one of the toughest things to surrender. Even Jesus said, "Truly, I say to you, it is hard for a rich man to enter the kingdom of heaven. Again I say to you, it is easier for a camel to go through the eye of a needle, than for a rich man to enter the kingdom of God." (Matthew 19:23-24)

In his book *The Hole in Our Gospel*, Richard Stearns tells the story of his own challenges as he struggled with the change God was calling him to. As a successful CEO and model Christian in his community he was called to leave it all behind to become the President of World Vision.

Read and reflect on his story.

The day I committed my life to Christ, I understood what it meant – following Christ no matter what. I was determined to not become one of those hypocrites who talked the talk but didn't walk the walk. After Renee and I married, she and I worked together to live intentionally for

Christ. We moved to Boston and showed up at Park Street Church on the Boston Common that very first Sunday. We led the kids' youth group, tithed our income faithfully, and got involved in Bible studies and fellowship groups whenever we could. Park Street was an amazing "missions church," and Renee and I eagerly attended every annual missions conference, giving our money liberally to support the cause. We were excited about spreading the good news about Christ across the world. I even became the church's youngest elder, at age twenty-seven. And at work, as I started my climb up the corporate ladder, I witnessed to people unashamedly and never shrank from an argument about faith or Christianity. In fact, when I was twenty-six and working at Parker Brothers (yes, the Monopoly, Clue, and Nerf Ball manufacturer), I almost got fired for leaving an hour early every Friday afternoon to work with the kids at our church. (summarized)

Renee enrolled in law school at Boston College, determined to follow her own dream to help the poor with their legal problems. With our first baby, Sarah, in tow, she graduated with distinction, passed the bar, and began serving the poor in rural Massachusetts. Our marriage, family, church involvement, and jobs were completely integrated with our understanding of what it meant to follow Jesus. So how did it happen that twenty years later I found myself weeping in my pj's, with the covers pulled over my head and begging God to let me off the hook? [2]

He goes on to explain the struggle that we all face when asked to give up what we believe to be ours for God had called him to leave Corporate America in order to lead a Christian non-profit organization.

Matthew makes this point very clear. A follower of Christ must surrender their possessions to Him.

As tough as this decision is, it must be made because it reveals the true intentions and condition of our heart. The desire for "more" and the illusion of security as a result of possessions will always be a battle, but a decision must be made in your heart today, will you surrender your possessions? In doing so, does that mean that you are choosing to live a life of poverty? Honestly, it's being willing to, if that is what He wants. But He may not have that in His plans for you.

In the Bible, you will find story after story where God chooses to give people wealth. In cases such as these, He does this so that those people can be used by Him to promote His kingdom and give Him glory.

In the Old Testament Abraham, Job, David, and Solomon, were all very wealthy individuals. Their wealth was used by God to carry out His plan on earth. David contributed much of his money to the building of God's temple. Solomon's wealth and fame became known around the world and people sought after him for his wisdom, the wisdom that God Himself gave him. Job had riches, lost it all, and gained in back two fold because of his faithfulness to God and because God wanted to prove a point.

In the New Testament, wealthy individuals supported the work of the Church and its missionaries like Paul. Others paid for Luke to research and document the life of Christ and the early Church which resulted in the books of Luke and Acts. The Magi brought luxurious gifts to Jesus as a child while another rich man provided the tomb that Jesus was buried in. We read about men and women who gave generously and are honored because of it.

We never see praise for the man or woman who hoards his or her wealth for personal pleasure, security, or worth.

Matthew himself was faced with this challenge and experienced this radical change. He was a wealthy tax collector. Yet he gave it all up to become a follower of Jesus Christ.

Many times, Jesus' disciples went with little or no food, had no place to stay, and were commanded to take nothing with them on their trips. In all circumstances, they were to trust God for every provision they needed.

Whether you are rich or poor, the fact remains true for a follower of Jesus Christ, what you own is not your own. We are to hold loosely to all God has given us, knowing that it could all be gone tomorrow. And if it is gone tomorrow, would that be okay? The answer to that question reveals what is in your heart; whether or not you have possessions or the possessions have you.

Jesus said it best:

> *"For what will it profit a man if he gains the whole world and forfeits his soul? Or what will a man give in exchange for his soul?"*
>
> *– Matthew 6:26*

Matthew understood this proposition. He knew the cost firsthand.

Perhaps the most meaningful lesson for me on this subject came when I visited India in 1994. While traveling on a summer mission trip we spent just over a week ministering in the slums of Bombay (now Mumbai). We stayed at the YMCA downtown and would take daily trips to visit a small church where we held Vacation Bible School and played with the children.

I remember it well. The smells were horrific as garbage and trash were piled on the sidewalks. Human dung lined the roadways next to the slums that had no plumbing or proper sewage lines. Those roadsides were washed clean (if you can call it that) by the monsoon rain as water 12 to 24 inches deep flooded the streets with its eerie and disgusting brown color.

Yet in this filth, poverty, and stench we found bright smiles on innocent faces, gleaming eyes of hope, and joyful sounds that filled their small meeting places. The chalky walls of one of the churches would discolor my hand as though wiping it on a chalkboard because of the humidity and poor quality paint. Yet in that paint were scripted the following words, "Thank you Lord Jesus for our many blessings."

Here the homeless, the outcast, and the forgotten found joy, not in what they possessed, but in Whose possession they were. They knew they belonged to God.

12 PRINCIPLES OF FOLLOW ME

I'll never forget the lesson I learned; all that I have and all that I possess is for His glory and no matter how much I have on this earth, my possessions cannot bring me the satisfaction, security, or the peace I desire. That joy and hope can only be found in letting go of all I have by giving it over to God, who is the Creator and Sustainer of all things.

When we give up control of our money and possessions we are letting God into every part of our lives. As a follower of Jesus, this is not an option or a suggestion. Everything we have is His, and by giving it up to Him, we are giving back to Him what is already His.

As a husband and as the provider for my family, I know this is hard. It's hard to continually trust God with the finances. It's not always easy to write a tithe check, or to give to someone in need when we have bills and expenses that need to be covered. But I must continually remind myself to let go and to trust God.

When I don't let go and when I seek to control it, I am no longer trusting God. When that happens I miss out on the blessings of seeing my Father provide for me and my family. Only He can provide security. Besides, I have to ask myself, "What would it profit me if I gain the whole world and yet forfeit my soul?"

3

Principle of Power

When you follow Christ, you have a change in power.

"Jesus summoned His twelve disciples and gave them authority over unclean spirits, to cast them out, and to heal every kind of disease and every kind of sickness."

— Matthew 10:1

"But you will receive power when the Holy Spirit has come upon you; and you shall be My witnesses both in Jerusalem, and in all Judea and Samaria, and even to the remotest part of the earth."

— Acts 2:8

Will power is the power to will oneself to do something that you don't want to do, or to continue doing something you love to do; the former being the more difficult to master. Whether it is dieting or abstaining from some form of addiction, the will to do something repeatedly without deviation, often fails. Yet our society teaches that each of us has the strength deep within us to make any desired change. Books, lectures, classes, videos, and more, line the shelves at book stores promoting ways that you can help yourself. Self-help is popular and feeds into the belief that the strongest source of power comes from somewhere within your own body.

Placing your security in your own power and strength, however, is like placing all your trust in the power utility company. It is true that power companies are dependable and fairly constant as they provide power to all the modern conveniences we enjoy. The cup of coffee I am enjoying right now as I write this was made possible by my utility company because it powered my one-cup coffee maker.

Every once in a while, however, there are major power outages.

It's in those times that you realize that the power company has limitations of its own. In parts of the country where power outages are common, people have alternative sources of energy. Some buy back-up generators, while others use propane gas. Still others simply have wood burning stoves to heat their homes and cook their food. Cities and States have entire disaster relief emergency plans in place for large scale power outages and other natural disasters. We know that all sources of energy have limitations and we plan for it so that eventually when they do run out we can replenish it or find a viable alternative.

Placing your security in anything that has been created by God (including your own will power, instead of God Himself) will eventually let you down. You, in your own strength, will eventually come to a point where you fail. Your own power will fail you.

We all know this to be true because we have all let ourselves down at one point or another. Simply put, we just can't keep it all together and be perfect all the time. No matter how many self-help books we read, there are times when we just simply fail. And there are times when circumstances out of our control change the direction of our life forever.

That's what Levi discovered. He had his life all figured out. His power came in the form of the money he collected and the position he held. His money, his plan, his profession, his strength was all he needed. He knew that people feared him and many hated him, but he knew the power he possessed was enough to keep him safe and secure. It all changed one day when he met Jesus.

The day Jesus entered Levi's life he realized that his own power was not enough. He could have continued down the path he was on, becoming a self-made man of wealth and power, but he didn't. He gave up his power to take on the power that Jesus offered him.

It is interesting to note that from the outside perspective, looking at his life, he had it all together. He didn't appear to need help. He didn't appear to be seeking something different. His actions, however, showed that he was seeking something different.

Paul, who once persecuted early Christians in his own power, also had a radical encounter with Jesus that changed his life forever.

From the outside, Paul also had it all together. He was a powerful force in his religious party. He was educated, trusted, and found favor with the leaders who endorsed his plans to stamp out the movement that Jesus had started.

While traveling on one of his trips to capture, torture, kill, and imprison Christians, Paul came face-to-face with Jesus, who confronted him about his plans (Acts 9). After Jesus reveals Himself to Paul, he immediately sees the error of his ways and becomes a follower of Christ. (If you haven't read the account of Paul's conversion, please take the time to read it in Acts.)

After Paul's conversion, he went on to be the greatest evangelist and missionary to the Gentiles in the first century. He wrote dozens of letters to the churches that he started. Over and over again, he writes that he did not preach in his own power, but by the power of the Holy Spirit. He recognized the limitations of his own strength and clung to the power of God.

In Romans Chapter 7:15-25, Paul writes to the church in Rome and explains the anguish a person feels when trying to live the perfect life in their own power.

> *For what I am doing, I do not understand; for I am not practicing what I would like to do, but I am doing the very thing I hate. But if I do the very thing I do not want to do, I agree with the Law, confessing that the Law is good. So now, no longer am I the one doing it, but sin which*

dwells in me. For I know that nothing good dwells in me, that is, in my flesh; for the willing is present in me, but the doing of the good is not. For the good that I want, I do not do, but I practice the very evil that I do not want. But if I am doing the very thing I do not want, I am no longer the one doing it, but sin which dwells in me.

I find then the principle that evil is present in me, the one who wants to do good. For I joyfully concur with the law of God in the inner man, but I see a different law in the members of my body, waging war against the law of my mind and making me a prisoner of the law of sin which is in my members. Wretched man that I am! Who will set me free from the body of this death? Thanks be to God through Jesus Christ our Lord! So then, on the one hand I myself with my mind am serving the law of God, but on the other, with my flesh the law of sin.

In the end, we are powerless. We don't really have power over the sins that rule our lives without the help of Christ and the Holy Spirit.

Jesus Himself gave us the best example of where we are to get our power.

Christ spent many sleepless nights in prayer with His Father asking for strength and courage to endure the future God had for Him. His life was the toughest of all lives, and He needed power from His Father in heaven.

If Christ, being fully divine, needed time with His Father, praying and seeking strength, direction, and wisdom from Him, how much more do we, being fully human, need time with our Father to deepen our faith and trust in Him?

We must seek God for power to accomplish anything. All things, great and small, are to be accomplished only by the power of God. When we achieve success in our own strength, we do so without the blessing of God. When we accumulate accolades and rewards for hard work without the power from the Spirit, we may earn the earthly praises, but we have lost the praise of our Father.

As a Christ follower, we must lay aside our rights and allow God to have the power and the authority. We must give Him the power of control over our lives, and the power within our lives so that we can live completely for Him and through Him. We cannot please God by doing anything in our own power.

The power we need comes from walking in the power of the Holy Spirit. Every person, when they decide to become a follower of Christ Jesus, is given the "gift" of the Holy Spirit. That means that God's Spirit is now living in you to give you power; power to live in obedience to Him. We can and will still sin and try to do things on our own, but we are supposed to give Him full authority over our lives. When we give Him authority, and then walk in obedience in His power, we begin to see change in our lives. That change is only possible by giving up our own power!

Unlike the power company that is prone to failure, the power He offers us is constant. Like a light bulb, we simply need to be plugged in and then we need to have the switch turned on to show its effect. Let go and let God flip the switch in your life. Let Him have His way and watch how you will shine!

A true follower of Jesus Christ *will* relinquish that power and control. Unfortunately many wait until they have exhausted all their resources and have nowhere else to turn. When they reach that point, they finally run to God.

Living life that way is exhausting and draining. Why do we do that?

Now is the time to ask God for His power and to give up your own in exchange for His. His power is never failing and will always sustain you no matter what you face in life. His power will provide wisdom and direction. His power is the never ending resource that you need right now, and in every moment of every day.

Jesus said it best when He taught "apart from Me, you can do nothing" (John 15:5).

Not only is His power needed for this life, it is also needed for the life to come.

Before Covid-19 spread throughout the world, a friend of mine passed away. A few days before his passing, he and his business partner had just had a talk about where their business was going and how excited they were about life in general. When we heard the news that he died in his sleep, we were all shocked. What went wrong?

He was only 45 years old. He was working on improving his health by eating better, working out four times a week, and he was making progress. He wasn't in "bad" shape before, but he wanted to be healthier, in better shape, and have more energy.

During the week before his death, he was fighting a head cold and a cough. The night before his death he went to bed very early from sheer exhaustion. At 4am his family checked on him because they heard him coughing. He told them he was okay and they all went back to sleep. When his car was still in the driveway at 8am they checked his room. It had been quiet and they didn't hear any coughing. Tragically, they found him on the floor unresponsive. The unimaginable had happened and we lost a great friend.

No matter how much we try to control the outcome, we are ultimately powerless over the days we have on earth.

As a Christ follower, it is time to let go of your power source, whatever that may be, and plug into His. It is not by your own strength or might or ability that will get you through this life. It is His power alone.

4

Principle of Position

When you follow Christ, you experience a change in position.

"So the last will be first, and the first will be last."

– Matthew 20:16

There is an old saying that says "unless you are the lead dog, the scenery never changes." The saying summarizes the driving spirit behind most of our lives. We desire to be at the head of the pack, the top dog, the head honcho, the top of the class. Our culture idolizes those that have achieved the pinnacles of success. Musicians and actors are idolized and every move they make is closely documented by paparazzi and displayed on magazine covers in the aisle of the grocery stores. Successful CEOs are sought after for advice and are asked to sit as members on various Boards of Directors where their wisdom and skills and power can be used to the benefit of others. We track these people and long to have the prestige that these people hold because of their positions…that is until they fall.

Why do we do that? Why do we idolize a few and ignore the rest? Do we long for what they have and how they live? Do we want to be them and in their positions? Do we ever truly get to know these people, or are they just words and pictures on a page?

We change our opinions so quickly when a person stumbles and falls from the top positions they once held. The drug addicted actor, the unscrupulous CEO who is facing criminal charges for fraud, the politician that has an affair, the athlete caught using illegal muscle enhancing drugs...and the list goes on.

Matthew teaches us that our position in this life is not what truly matters. Jesus clearly taught that the Kingdom of Heaven belonged to the weak, meek, humble, and the children. Not to the powerful, rich, and famous.

It is human nature to choose leaders based on outer appearances. Even King David's own father overlooked him because he was the youngest (and probably not the handsomest). Nothing has changed since then. It's even more obvious today that people who are handsome and beautiful, tall and fit, great orators, or people with outgoing personalities and charisma are often selected for powerful and influential positions. These men and women seemingly have no weaknesses whatsoever and they go to great lengths to hide any flaws.

We know, however, that the Bible tells us that one day the weak and the lowly will be raised up and the humbled exalted, while the proud and the rich will be brought low. The powerless martyrs who lost their lives for Christ's sake at the hands of someone else who had the position of power will be rewarded for giving their lives.

When we encounter Christ and choose to follow Him, we realize that to follow means we must live as Jesus did. That means we become a servant.

Matthew takes us all the way back to the prophet Isaiah in the Old Testament where he describes the character traits of the Messiah. In Isaiah 42:1, God described Jesus when He said, "Behold, my servant..." (Matthew 12:18). Even before

Jesus was born, it was planned that He would be a servant. Let me say that again, He is a servant.

Days before His own death, we see Jesus kneeling before His own friends and disciples…even the one who will betray Him that night. He is washing their dirt encrusted feet with His very own hands (John 13:5-17).

This act of servitude was unheard of in its day. The teacher would never bow to the student, or the leader to the servant, or a father to his child. A Jewish slave would not even be asked to wash the feet of another Jew. Yet, it is here that we find Jesus in the lowliest of places.

When Jesus does this, He is giving us a true picture of subordination of power. Peter, one of the disciples, even forbids Him from washing his feet, and then relents after Jesus explains that the washing is symbolic of the internal spiritual change that takes place when we choose to follow Christ.

As followers of Christ, we are washed clean by our Savior. His act of service to these men symbolized this fact. When Jesus willfully laid down His life as a sacrifice for our sins, He served us in a manner that no other person could. He served His followers in life and in death.

A follower of Christ who seeks a position of power based on skills, talents, money, and other humanly measurable accolades in their own strength with their own agendas does so without the blessings of Christ. He or she may succeed from a human perspective, but fail from a spiritual one.

Pete McKenzie, a pastor and mentor of mine often says, "A servant with their own agenda is no servant at all and is worthless." In other words, we cannot call ourselves servants of Christ if we have our own agendas.

We are called to be servants to God and others. We often come to God, however, willing to serve, but with our own agenda and on our own terms. We offer to serve Him, as long He does not send us to a foreign land, make us clean toilets, or spend time with the homeless.

We offer to give money to churches and other ministries, even the poor, so long as we have enough to keep for ourselves to remain secure.

We are willing to entertain the change of position so long as it's not too inconvenient.

Sadly, we offer only part of ourselves because we don't trust that He truly knows best and then blame God when everything in our life falls apart.

I have found that I'll gladly surrender control in specific areas of my life, only after I have exhausted all my options. As self-sufficient humans, we think we don't need to surrender when things are going well and then change our minds when things start to unravel.

Take work, for example. We hold onto the reins at work, justifying our claim on our position because it's going well and it's all under control. Our marriage, on the other hand, may be falling apart and because we don't know how to fix it, we surrender that to God. On one hand, we keep one area of our life under our control because we think we can manage and handle it while surrendering another area we know we cannot fix. We pick and choose what or where we will surrender and what we will not. We can't do that. We need to surrender every area of our life and recognize that God has so much more for us if we give Him all control.

When I talk with other believers about life circumstances I often find myself saying, "It's all in God's hands." If we are honest with ourselves, what we are really saying is that we are willing to give God the parts of our lives we feel we have no control over. We aren't really giving Him everything, just the parts we can't control ourselves.

Levi had a powerful position as a tax collector for the Roman government. He enjoyed wealth and physical protection from the Romans. Although he was hated by his fellow Jews, his position was secure. When he answered Jesus' call to "follow Me" he left his position and status behind. His wealth and protection were all abandoned as he placed his trust in Jesus and in Him alone.

Jesus calls us to abandon our rights to our positions. He may not call us to give up the positions He has placed us in, but He calls us to give up our rights to them. He is the one that places leaders in leadership positions, and He can take those positions away if He sees a better plan for that leader or a better plan for His followers.

I have to continually surrender my rights so that He can have His way. Is it easy? No way. I have to work on it every day and often don't even realize that I've taken back the reins to my life. Then something happens to me that reveals I have repositioned myself into the driver's seat. At that point, I must surrender again.

An authentic follower of Jesus Christ must settle this issue in their heart at some point. Like Richard Stearns, many don't even realize they have not surrendered their position until they are faced with the challenge of giving up what they have accumulated for themselves.

Surrendering your rights to your position is not easy and it will be a challenge you face your entire life. But we must continually lay down our rights to ourselves and our positions as His faithful followers and give up all control and surrender to God.

It is in surrendering that we can find true peace, contentment, and joy as we allow God to work in our hearts and lives.

5

Principle of Perspective

When you follow Christ, you have a change in perspective.

"Then Jesus said to His disciples, 'If anyone wishes to come after Me, he must deny himself, and take up his cross and follow Me. For whoever wishes to save his life will lose it; but whoever loses his life for My sake will find it.'"

— Matthew 16:24-25

"And the disciples came and said to Him, 'Why do You speak to them in parables?' Jesus answered them, 'To you it has been granted to know the mysteries of the kingdom of heaven, but to them it has not been granted.'"

— Matthew 13:11-11

"And Jesus said to him, 'Blessed are you, Simon Barjona, because flesh and blood did not reveal this to you, but My Father who is in heaven.'"

– Matthew 16:17

Imagine a world without the satellite images of the Earth, Google Earth doesn't exist, and no one has ever traveled far from home. What would your perspective of Earth be? How would you draw a map of the world? Some people believed the world was flat and believed that if you were to sail a ship too far out into the ocean, you were going to fall off the end of the earth. Others, however, observed the stars and other astronomical events and determined that the world was round.

As early as the 6th century BC, we see the idea of a round earth taking shape in ancient Greek sources. By 240 BC, Eratosthenes estimated the earth's circumference using trigonometry and the angles of shadows cast in two different cities. His measurement was within 5% of the real size.[3] He did that without computers or calculators!

Gradually, the belief that the earth was round spread throughout the ancient world, and by the time Jesus came, it was well spread and generally accepted to be true.

It's hard for us to imagine what it must have been like to think differently about the world and its shape. But let's try. Put yourself in the past, in their time of history, and pretend you believe the world is flat. Now imagine what it would be like to sit around the fire and hear stories from your parents, uncles, and grandparents. Stories of people trying to measure the earth's circumference, or saying that the constellations were different in other parts of the world at the same time of the year. How would you know if they were correct? Your perspective would have been shaped by your upbringing and your own personal experiences. In reality, we all get comfortable with our own perspectives and opinions and resist new ideas that conflict with our own. It is likely you'd hear those stories and think of them as fables.

What would have happened, however, if while living during that time, you had the opportunity to travel up into the sky and bring back a recorded image of the earth from outer space? Wouldn't that radically change your perspective immediately without question? Your whole life would change. Your perspective and understanding would have been forever changed.

There are times in our lives when we have a paradigm shift in our thinking. This happened to me when I became a father for the very first time. Our first child went into breach about a month before he was due. After a failed attempt to right the baby, we scheduled a c-section. Were it not for modern medicine, I might not be a father or a husband.

Upon the arrival of my son, my view of the world and where I placed my priorities changed. When we go through that kind of circumstance and life change, what we believed to be true at one point, is replaced by a new thought or belief after experiencing or discovering something that makes you question your first belief.

We've all heard familiar phrases like, "If it's gonna be, it's up to me!" and, "If you want it done the right way, do it yourself." At the root of sayings like these is a philosophy, or perspective about the world, that says we are in charge of our own destiny. We approach life with the hopes of gaining and achieving something more than we had in the past. We are driven to greatness and feel the need to leave a legacy. But how do we gauge our success? How do we truly know if what we are doing is the right thing? What if it's not?

Mark Mittelberg, in his book *Choosing Your Faith...In a World of Spiritual Options* points out that many rely solely on "feelings and intuition" to determine their perspective on life and spiritual matters and goes on to say that what you feel may not necessarily be real or right or good.[4] In essence, he was saying that we can't always trust that our perspective is the right perspective and we must test that perspective against other evidence to see if our feelings and intuition are valid. Wouldn't it be horrible to climb the ladder of success only to find out that it's leaning on the wrong wall, or even the wrong building altogether?

Before Matthew decided to follow Christ Jesus he had a certain perspective on life that made it possible for him to be a tax-collector. His life was radically changed when Jesus gave him a Kingdom perspective.

Matthew unveils paradox after paradox as he records Jesus' numerous teaching on the Kingdom of Heaven. For example, Jesus taught that the Kingdom of Heaven belongs to those who are poor in spirit (Matthew 5:3).

Be honest. Who, in their right mind, would agree with the statement that the Kingdom of Heaven belongs to the poor in spirit and that the meek are the ones who are blessed? Who would have thought that the greatest in God's Kingdom would actually be the least on the earth? Who would have thought that the Kingdom of God belongs to little children? Who would have thought that a widow giving her two pennies would be more honored than the one who gave thousands of dollars? Who would have thought this?

God did. And He uses Matthew to teach it to us.

Matthew records Jesus' teachings about life and the way that it really works. Without His help, we don't see it correctly. Even with His help, we still have difficulty seeing life the way it should be because we are human. Paul says that we see things dimly because although much has been revealed, there is still much more that hasn't been (1 Corinthians 13:12). God's word and His Spirit are given as counselors to help us understand that the measuring tools the world uses to gauge success are not the same as the ones God uses.

So what perspective does God want us to have? He wants us to have His perspective.

God has been working out His plan to save mankind from our sins from the very moment that Adam and Eve sinned. The death, burial, and resurrection of Jesus are the culmination of this plan the makes it possible for us to be saved from our sins and He wants us to follow Christ.

He wants us to understand that loving God and loving others is the most important thing that we can do.

He wants us to understand that if we only live for ourselves, we will lose our lives in the end. If we selfishly store up for ourselves the riches that we have amassed we will forfeit eternity with Him. If we neglect the needy and the poor we too will be neglected by the Father.

He wants us to understand that getting into heaven is not about the amount of good works we do. In fact, it's not about good works or deeds. It's about being in a relationship with the Creator of the universe made possible only through Christ.

Jesus teaches about the privilege of getting into heaven; that it's not reserved for those that feel they deserve it, but for those who know they don't. It's not for those that do miracles in the name of Jesus, but for those who can name Jesus as their personal Savior. It's not for those that have lived a good life, but for those who realize they have no good in them.

He wants us to understand that this life is not about us at all. The events of today are His plan working itself out. It's actually all about Him! It's not about you. As my professor at BIOLA once said, when we look at history, we realize that it is His Story, not ours.

A follower of Christ no longer asks, "What's in it for me?" Instead, he asks, "What's in it for the Kingdom?" We evaluate everything through this new perspective.

Paul experienced this change in his life when he was on the road to Damascus. Up until that point in his life he was zealous for persecuting Christians to stop the spread of this new sect that was threatening his core beliefs and values. He was ruthless until the day he encountered Jesus. After encountering Christ face-to-face his whole perspective on life changed. So drastic was the life change that it took years for the Christians to really trust that his life and mission truly had changed. No longer opposed to Christ, he was now willing to die for Christ and lived the rest of his life spreading the good news of the Gospel.

Each of us needs to experience this change of perspective. Followers of Christ go through this change and have radical eye-opening experiences as the Holy Spirit begins to reveal that which was formerly hidden.

A friend of mine explained to me that he didn't know that he didn't know that he was not a true follower of Jesus Christ until after he truly accepted Christ into his life. Let me say that again...he did not know that he didn't know!

He recalled how, for years, he attended church with his family because it was the "right" thing to do. Week after week he'd come to church, sit in the service, enjoy the sermon, give some money, and then leave. According to his perspective, he was doing pretty good. Then one day, he personally encountered Jesus for the first time, and his eyes were opened to the fact that he did not have a personal relationship with Him. It wasn't until he really knew Jesus that he realized that he hadn't known Him to begin with. All of the principles I've laid out in this book can be seen in his transformed life.

His life completely changed since the day Jesus gave him a new perspective.

Right now is the best time to slow down and reevaluate your perspective on life. Is it shaped by God's Word or the world? Ask God to reveal His perspective to you.

When your perspective changes you will find that those who do not know Jesus simply won't see things the same way you do. If you know Jesus, then you know this to already be true. Jesus taught that people who are not followers will not understand what or why true followers do what they do. In Matthew 13:14-17 we find this passage, left as an encouragement to all His followers when we see others walking blindly.

Therefore I speak to them in parables; because while seeing they do not see, and while hearing they do not hear, nor do they understand.

In their case the prophecy of Isaiah is being fulfilled, which says, 'YOU WILL KEEP ON HEARING, BUT WILL NOT UNDERSTAND; YOU WILL KEEP ON SEEING, BUT WILL NOT PERCEIVE; FOR THE HEART OF THIS PEOPLE HAS BECOME DULL,

WITH THEIR EARS THEY SCARCELY HEAR,

AND THEY HAVE CLOSED THEIR EYES,

OTHERWISE THEY WOULD SEE WITH THEIR EYES, HEAR WITH THEIR EARS, AND UNDERSTAND WITH THEIR HEART AND RETURN, AND I WOULD HEAL THEM.'

But blessed are your eyes, because they see; and your ears, because they hear. For truly I say to you that many prophets and righteous men desired to see what you see, and did not see it, and to hear what you hear, and did not hear it.

What a privilege it is to know that I, a follower of Jesus, have been given eyes to see, and ears to hear. It is impossible to follow Christ without having a change of perspective on the way life works and how we fit into God's plan for us and this world.

.

6

Principle of Priorities

A follower of Christ will have a change in priorities.

"For where your treasure is, there your heart will be also."

– Matthew 6:21

"For it is written, 'You shall worship the LORD your God, and serve Him only.'"

– Matthew 4:10b

As we discussed previously, when we have a change of perspective, it changes our lives in many ways. One of the ways our lives change is that our lives are centered on new priorities.

It is common for individuals and families to have changes in priorities when they know in advance that their lives are coming to an end. A family I know changed their priorities when their one year old was diagnosed with brain cancer. For the next three years they fought the cancer, seeking every form of treatment known to offer hope. When they knew that there was nothing more that they could do, they focused on creating great memories for the rest of their children. They pulled the kids out of school and took a last minute trip to Hawaii. After all, is school that important when you know your younger brother is going to be gone soon? Everyone in the family had a change of priorities.

Another friend of mine, a mom with two boys under the age of two, went to the hospital for abdominal pain. The doctors had diagnosed her with appendicitis and were going to remove the appendix. After further testing they discovered that she had stage three colon cancer, not appendicitis. Together, she and her husband, and their family are now focused on medical treatments and doctor follow up visits. Their lives will never be the same.

Those who are on their deathbeds, or nearing the end of their lives, often get their estates in order. Wills and plans are drawn up so that the families can carry out their wishes. When a parent dies, children make it a priority to carry out those wishes. It's never convenient, but it's a priority, and it gets done.

How we spend our time and what we spend our time on reveals our priorities. Time itself is the biggest indicator of what is important to you. No one wants to "waste" time, so it's clear that whatever we do, we feel as though it's a good use of our time.

When counseling with a friend, I encouraged him to spend more time in prayer and reading the Bible.

"I just don't have enough time." was his response.

"You don't have enough time?" I pressed.

"Well..." you know the rest of the story. He had plenty of time for other things but could not find the time to read the Bible on a daily basis.

The truth is that we spend time on things that we treasure. If we treasure fun and pleasure we spend time seeking out fun and pleasure. If we treasure relaxation we pursue the absence of activity. If we treasure entertainment we will spend a lot of time watching YouTube, Netflix, and movies or go to concerts and events. If we are pursuing retirement we spend time working a little harder and longer now to achieve that goal sooner, if possible.

Matthew had a goal at one time. As a tax-collector, there were plans in place that would allow him to eventually retire. Perhaps he had dreams of having a vacation home away from the city where he could relax and enjoy life. Whether or not that was the case, we'll never know; but we do know that his priority was wrapped up in himself and his plans for his family. Why else would a person take on a job that was hated by his fellow countrymen? He did it because he believed the benefits far outweighed the drawbacks. When Christ called him, however, his priorities changed. He became a Christ follower and spent time with his Savior carrying out His will instead of collecting taxes.

It's not really hard to figure out where your priorities are. A quick glance at your calendar will reveal this. We put what is important to us on the calendar. We make time for activities that we want to participate in. If a total stranger were to find your calendar, would they know you are a follower of Christ, simply by the entries? Would they see time for studying God's Word, prayer, fasting, fellowship, and other activities that nourish your soul and your relationship with Christ and other Christ followers? Spending time in God's Word and prayer don't happen by chance. You have to choose to do them and make time for them.

Another way to look at your priorities is to evaluate what you do when you have nothing to do? What do you do between the events logged in your weekly schedule? What fills in those gaps? TV, Facebook, Instagram, YouTube, Pinterest, reading the paper, dining out, exercising, working in the garage on a project, sleeping, Candy Crush, or debating political views online? The list is endless and your answer will reveal the priorities in your life.

I struggle with this when I am tired after a long day of work. I'm exhausted and want to disengage and just vegetate for a little while. It's so easy to just turn on the TV, or pick up the iPad and watch meaningless shows or play games. That's what our culture has become accustomed to because that is what's easy. But I must ask myself...does God have a better plan for me?

After a long day of ministry Jesus was exhausted. When that happened, he would withdraw to a quiet place to spend time with His Father. His priority was to know His Father's will by spending time with Him in prayer.

After accepting Christ's invitation, Matthew spent time with Jesus and then dedicated much of his time to writing. He gathered data and wrote down, by the power of the Holy Spirit, the Gospel of Matthew, which serves as the introduction to the New Testament. From tax collector to God's writer; now that's what I call a change in priorities. And why did he do it? Not for the money or for the fame, but to preserve the teachings of Jesus so others would be able to understand that Jesus is the Son of God, the One and only Messiah, the promised One of the Old Testament, the Savior of our souls.

Another change in priorities is reflected in how we use the skills and talents God has given us. Obviously Matthew, being a tax collector, was very good with numbers. Is it any wonder that numbers are significant to him and how he arranged his writings and teachings of Jesus? There are seven sermons, seven mountains, 5,000 are fed in one story, 4,000 in another, etc. Clearly, he allowed God to use his talents to record the teachings of Jesus in such a powerful way.

What unique talents has God given you? Are you a great speaker, teacher, writer, or do you have a heart of compassion? Are you using your talents to advance His kingdom?

When I was about 10 years old, my grandfather, a peach and nectarine farmer in the San Joaquin Valley of California, taught me a lesson I have never forgotten. In fact, I remember it like it was yesterday. One day, I was being nosey and was going through his desk drawer in his office where I stumbled across his checkbook. He saw me with it in my hands and in his wisdom he said to me, "You show me a man's checkbook, and I'll show you his heart." He knew what I'd find in the pages of his checkbook.

My grandfather had a wealth of talents and skills when it came to fruit farming. He worked hard, dropping out of college to return to the family business when his dad got sick. He used his knowledge of farming to teach his grandkids, and others, the truths found in Scripture, especially the parts about God's discipline and pruning and how pruning is necessary for better fruit.

He was a living example to me and the other grandkids and taught us about faithfully trusting God, about being generous, righteous living, loving and caring for his wife, faithful church attendance, and how donuts on a Saturday morning after a sleepover only came after prayer and the reading of God's word.

Throughout the years he trusted God. He was a faithful servant doing his part, trusting that God would do His part. Some years were great, most were not. But his faith never wavered. Never stingy, he was always generous, and in the end when he went to be with Jesus, he left enough money for my grandmother to live comfortably so that she would not have to worry about finances.

But what I remember about that day when I was going through his checkbook was how many checks were written out to his church and the missionary organizations that they supported. Here was a lowly and humble farmer giving away so much money. Even as a child I was amazed.

My grandpa taught by example that our time, talents, and money goes toward things that we hold dear. As a follower of Christ, we have to turn those over to God and say to Him, "What I have is Yours. Use it as You see fit. Help me to place a priority on the things in the world that are most important to You." After all, shouldn't we be able to trust the Creator of the universe to help us prioritize every part of our lives?

In August of 2013 I had the opportunity to travel to Hyderabad India with Friends Church Yorba Linda as an ongoing part of our partnership with Operation Mobilization (OM) India to help build schools for the Dalits. This trip was particularly special to me because I was blessed to be able to visit the MBC Bible College in Shamshabad Hyderabad with my son. The school campus is located about an hour south of downtown Hyderabad in a rural area that is being quickly developed as a result of the Indian government relocating their international airport less than five miles away.

When I was growing up I would visit my Grandma Grace's home and see pictures and artifacts from India and would eat curried chicken. She would tell us stories about her childhood growing up "over there" and I was fascinated by them. I knew that my great grandparents had spent time as Missionaries there and that my grandma was born in India. What I didn't know until my trip to the campus was that my great-great grandparents had traveled to India in 1899 and helped start the mission outpost that is now known as the MBC Bible College. My grandma was born in a home located on that very plot of land and my son and I were able to see the room where she was likely born. We also saw photos of my ancestors in photo albums they had stored at the college. I was in awe. 114 years after my family settled there and established a medical missionary outpost, my son and I were spending time in India, falling in love with and serving the same people, in the exact same spot they settled.

Over a century ago, as Christ followers, my ancestors had a change of priorities that took them halfway around the globe to translate the Bible into the local Telugu language and to educate the people. Their willingness to go brought about a legacy that still continues. Men from all over the country come to the MBC Bible College Seminary to study God's Word and return to their churches to teach and pastor their churches. On this trip I was able to experience first-hand God's faithfulness to my family and to the people of India because of their priorities.

I ask you the same question that I had to ask myself while in India, *"What will I be remembered for 114 years from now?"* Will you be remembered for something great or something awful or will you simply be forgotten? My son Levi was the 6th generation family member to visit India for the cause of Christ. What will the 6th generation in my family line be doing? I pray they will be serving Christ and remembering me as an avid Christ follower who made it my priority to serve Jesus faithfully as well.

7

Principle of Plans

When you follow Christ, you have a change in plans.

> *"Immediately they left the boat and their father, and followed Him."*
>
> — *Matthew 4:22*

> *"Now listen, you who say, 'Today or tomorrow we will go to this or that city, spend a year there, carry on business and make money.' Why, you do not even know what will happen tomorrow. What is your life? You are a mist that appears for a little while and then vanishes."*
>
> — *James 4:13-14*

The way of a fool is right in his own eyes, But a wise man is he who listens to counsel.

– Proverbs 2:15

Every child is asked, "What do you want to be when you grow up?" and is expected to have an answer by the time they graduate from high school. After all, isn't it the American Dream to go on to "bigger" and "better" things? When a student enters college, they need to declare a major so that they can pick the right classes and get on the right path to a timely graduation.

When a person graduates from college they are expected to pursue that goal and dream because they have already worked so hard to get to the place where they are at. To do otherwise would just be "throwing it all away". This is all in answer to that very innocent question, "What do you want to be?"

Everyone has a plan; some just have more clarity than others about what this plan looks like. There are thousands of young entrepreneurs working around the clock trying to produce the next "Facebook" or "Google" that will have a public IPO and make them billionaires. Others may not have that kind of clarity and are still trying to figure it out.

Our culture teaches us that we are supposed to have a goal or dream, then make a plan to execute it. There are 90-day plans, the 1 year plan, the 5 year plan, the 10 year plan, the investment plan, and the retirement plan. Plan, plan, plan! It's what we are taught to do so that every step we make can be measured against our plans. Failure to execute the plan is a disaster waiting to happen.

When we decide to surrender our lives to Christ and follow Him, we also surrender our plans.

We no longer ask the question, "What do I want to be when I grow up?" Now, we ask the question, "What do You want me to be?" God created you and you are His prized creation. He has a great plan for you based on the way He created you!

Turning over your plans to God can be scary if you have been clinging tightly to them your entire life. But once you realize that the God who created you has a wonderful plan for you it brings comfort and peace.

Ephesians 2:10 says:

> *"For we are His workmanship, created in Christ*
> *Jesus for good works, which God prepared*
> *beforehand so that we would walk in them."*

The word "workmanship" is the Greek word for poem. Our lives are to be like a beautifully written poem that resembles poetry in motion. And what are we called to do? Good works! That's God's plan for all of us; that our lives would be a beautiful example of good works for His glory.

Before surrendering to Christ, your plan is solely focused on what you can accomplish in your own timing, skills, and determination. After surrendering to Christ, the plan is now focused on what God wants to accomplish through you.

Personally, I have found that God's plans are much more satisfying than my own. When your plans and God's plans align, that's where you experience peace. Your life may be falling apart physically, yet you can still have His peace.

Matthew's plan was to make enough money tax-collecting so that he could eventually retire. As I conjectured previously, he may have even had dreams of retiring in a vacation home opposite the Jordan River away from the city. That all changed on the day when he decided to follow Christ.

Many Christians will tell you that God has big plans for your life, but then fail to tell you how to discover those plans. Over the years I have learned a lot about discovering God's will for my life.

When I was younger, I was struggling with a career decision. I didn't know if I should pursue a full-time position in the ministry or a "secular" career outside of the Church. I grew up thinking that if I wanted to make God truly happy with me, that I needed to be in full-time ministry. I had graduated from BIOLA University with a degree in Biblical and Theological studies but didn't have a clear direction for my life. Proverbs teaches that a wise person seeks counsel so I decided that I needed to seek counsel from men that I trusted.

One of the men I spoke to was an attorney who had previously been a pastor and I wanted to know more about his story and his decision to become an attorney. At our meeting he simply asked me a few questions:

1. Did I love Jesus with all my heart?

2. Was my priority to seek God's Kingdom over my own?

3. Was what I wanted to do illegal or contrary to any of God's Word?

I answered Yes, Yes, and No respectively. Then he told me to do whatever I wanted because God will use me wherever I am, no matter what I am doing. That lifted a real burden.

After taking steps to pursue ministry opportunities it became clear that God was closing the doors to that career path. Honestly, I don't know why He chose to do that, but I had to surrender that to Him and trust that He knows better than I do.

As a Christ follower, I earnestly desire His plan for my life. If that means working outside of the church in a "secular" job then He is pleased and supportive of that!

Over the years, various pastors I've sat under have taught on the topic of discovering God's will for our lives and have taught similar teachings about God's will. For some, after a decision has been made to follow Christ, there is a radical change in *what* that person does. It's like being on a sinking ship and finding a whole new ship to sail in. If you find yourself in this position, you may need to seek a new career.

For others it's a radical change in the *way* they do what they do. It's like a ship that changes course when the winds suddenly change. You may find that your job is in alignment with God's principles but you need to make changes to how you carry out your responsibilities. Rather than abandoning the ship you are sailing, you simply adjust your headings and you set sail in a new direction.

Whatever the case may be for your life, I believe that you will know what to do after seeking godly, Bible-based counsel, searching the Scriptures, and listening to the Holy Spirit. God promises to give wisdom to all who ask it and to provide His Spirit as a Counselor to guide us.

Surrendering our plans is not easy. It involves a change in our thinking and in the way we live life. Some changes can and will be costly and can threaten your source of income. Other changes will challenge your sense of worth within your social circles because a change of plans is something that can't be hidden and opens you up to public criticism which, at times, can hurt.

Joseph and Mary understood this. Mary, betrothed to Joseph, becomes pregnant. Can you imagine the embarrassment and the shame she felt? She left her family and went and stayed with her relative Elizabeth for months! Joseph, upon learning she was pregnant, planned to send her away because he did not want to disgrace her. God, however, sent his angel to direct their steps and encourage them during their difficult time.

We are encouraged over and over in the Bible to trust in God and His plans for our lives, not our own plans. The book of Proverbs is written so that those who read it might become wise and says that we should trust in God and not lean on our own understanding (3:5), that there is a way that seems right to us, but in the end it is the way of death (14:12), that it's better to have a little with righteousness than to have great income with injustice (16:8), that those who trust in the Lord will be blessed (16:20), and those who listen to Him will live securely (1:33), and promises that He will be a shield to those who walk with integrity (2:7).

Matthew records the lesson Jesus taught about two builders, one wise, the other foolish in Matthew 7:24-27. He taught that anyone who heard His teachings and acted upon them would be like the wise man who built his house upon the rock, providing a stable foundation for his building. When the rains, floods, and the winds slammed against the house, it did not fall.

The person who hears His words and does not act upon them will be like the foolish man who built his house on the sand. When the rain fell, and the floods came, and the winds blew and slammed against the house, it fell and it was a great fall.

It's important to note here that both the wise man and the foolish man built homes and faced the same storms. The difference is that the man who listened to and acted upon

Jesus' teachings was not destroyed in the storms of life. Just because you are following God's plans does not mean you won't have any troubles or problems. In fact, it's quite the contrary; you will have problems, troubles, and trials as you live out His plan for you. A person devoted to living out God's plans will be challenged. We all have to face consequences for bad decisions we've made in the past, and Satan is trying to steal away the seeds of faith that God sewed. We live in a fallen world where sinfulness impacts everything. Time and time again we see God's people suffering because of the consequences of sin in the world. Even Jesus suffered because of sin (not His), yet persevered through it and was victorious.

Jesus successfully carried out His Father's plan perfectly and is worthy of our trust. We can confidently commit our plans to Him. If you have not committed your plans to Him yet, I pray that you will today. God is good and His plans for us are awesome.

My prayer is that you don't put off the changes that you know you need to make. An authentic follower of Christ will do what God calls him or her to do no matter the consequences. Trust that God's plans for your life are better than your own. He is a God of love and wants you to truly know Him in every aspect of your life.

8

Principle of Practices

When you follow Christ, you have a change in practices.

"Therefore bear fruit in keeping with repentance; and do not suppose that you can say to yourselves, 'We have Abraham for our father'; for I say to you that from these stones God is able to raise up children to Abraham. The axe is already laid at the root of the trees; therefore every tree that does not bear good fruit is cut down and thrown into the fire."

–Matthew 3:8-10

*"When I was a child, I used to speak like a child,
think like a child, reason like a child; when I
became a man, I did away with childish things.
For now we see in a mirror dimly, then face to
face; now I know in part, but then I will know
fully just as I also have been fully known."*

—1 Corinthians 13:11-12

When I see someone who proclaims they are a Christian, but does not act like it, these are the phrases that come to my mind.

"Practice what you preach!"

"He's such a hypocrite!"

I'm sure you've thought the same.

As television shows have become more and more grotesque, vulgar, and fallen off the moral cliff, I've resorted to watching "Reality TV". Although it's not reality (I have family members in the entertainment industry who have shared some insight with me), I do get to see how people behave in various situations…usually strenuous ones. For the most part we get to see mostly unscripted dialogue between individuals and groups. Sadly, I cringe when they interview someone who boldly proclaims they are a Christian. Why? Because more often than not they go on to do something that does not line up with their proclamation or with God's Word. They lie, cheat, steal, and swear just like the rest of the people on the show. Or they whine and complain all the time, lose hope, and get into ridiculous arguments. In the end, they are not any different from the others except for the fact they say they are Christians.

Unfortunately, this duplicity is the reason many people who have observed Christians have chosen to disregard Christianity altogether. They are turned off by the hypocrisy in the Church and they see no difference between a "Christian" and a non-Christian. This is very sad, yet true.

There are some parents that raise their kids with this philosophy, "Do as I say, not as I do." Essentially, they are agreeing with the fact that there are a set of ideals that should be held to, but in reality they are not holding to these ideals themselves. A simple example is when a parent lies about their child's age when buying tickets to a theme park, movie, or other event in order to pay the lower fee. A true follower of Christ cannot have this double standard.

There is no way that a true follower can be satisfied with the status quo of living life the "old" way. The old way was characterized by sinful desires and motives; by anger, rage, malice, slander, filthy language, jealousy, bitterness, gossiping, disobedience, and other natural born tendencies. Once a decision has been made to follow Christ, there is going to be a change in the way life is lived.

Read Apostle Paul's words to the Christians at Colossae,

Therefore consider the members of your earthly body as dead to immorality, impurity, passion, evil desire, and greed, which amounts to idolatry. For it is because of these things that the wrath of God will come upon the sons of disobedience, and in them you also once walked, when you were living in them. But now you also, put them all aside: anger, wrath, malice, slander, and abusive speech from your mouth. Do not lie to one another, since you laid aside the old self with its evil practices, and have put on the new self who is being renewed to a true knowledge according to the image of the One who created him.

- Colossians 3:5-10

It's impossible to follow Christ without seeing a change in the way you live.

We've already discussed some of the changes in Matthew's life after choosing to follow Christ. In the book of Luke we see another tax collector who has a change in practices when he meets Jesus.

> *He [Jesus] entered Jericho and was passing through. And there was a man called by the name of Zaccheus; he was a chief tax collector and he was rich.*
>
> *Zaccheus was trying to see who Jesus was, and was unable because of the crowd, for he was small in stature. So he ran on ahead and climbed up into a sycamore tree in order to see Him, for He was about to pass through that way. When Jesus came to the place, He looked up and said to him, "Zaccheus, hurry and come down, for today I must stay at your house." And he hurried and came down and received Him gladly.*
>
> *When they saw it, they all began to grumble, saying, "He has gone to be the guest of a man who is a sinner." Zaccheus stopped and said to*

the Lord, "Behold, Lord, half of my possessions I will give to the poor, and if I have defrauded anyone of anything, I will give back four times as much." And Jesus said to him, "Today salvation has come to this house, because he, too, is a son of Abraham. For the Son of Man has come to seek and to save that which was lost."

- Luke 19:1-10

When he met Jesus, the way Zaccheus practiced life and business changed. Although Scripture does not say it, being that they were in the same profession, Matthew probably knew Zaccheus or knew of him and he could relate to his story because he had a similar experience with Jesus.

When Christ becomes the center focus of your life, your practices change. There is simply no way around it. You can't be like you once were and live like you once did and move forward in a true relationship with Jesus Christ. While the Holy Spirit works in you to convict you of sin and of righteousness you will see your life begin to change.

A friend of mine who has since passed away understood what this is like. He lived a life as a business executive, drawing a six figure salary, driving a nice car, living in a nice house, and living the dream.

From the outside he looked like he had it made. While he looked like he had it together on the outside, he was self-destructive on the inside. He had an addiction to drugs. His career drew him away from his family and the life he was living was headed for disaster. He lost his job, was unemployed, and came to a point in his life where he surrendered his life to Christ. On the day he committed to following Jesus, his entire life changed. God delivered him from his drug addictions and he never looked back.

The rest of his life, until the day he died, was radically different from before, clearly marked by his newfound relationship with Jesus. God chose to give him a new career. He started a singing ministry and became a missionary for Jesus, singing to the elderly at their care facilities, raising support for his expenses, living month-to-month, trusting Jesus to be his provider.

Countless lives have been changed because of his transformation. Many souls have been welcomed into heaven because of his love for others and his being there to share the gospel of Jesus Christ to them on their deathbeds.

When he finally let it all go, he came alive. He found the joy that he had been looking for. He found it after he lost everything he had worked so hard to gain when God changed his life.

Another friend of mine, Bill Kauble, attended Church every week with his wife and kids. "Why not go to church?" he thought. "After all, it's good to have God on my side too." So, week in and week out, year after year, he attended, sat in the comfortable seats, and then left quietly, rarely connecting with anyone. He did this for twelve years. But his life was a mess. He didn't truly know Christ and Christ didn't have an impact on the way he lived life.

It happened on a Sunday. He was at church with his family, like normal, when he realized for the first time in 12 years that he didn't truly know God, nor have a relationship with Jesus. The lifestyle he portrayed for those few hours on Sunday morning was not the same as the life he lived at work or at home.

Now, Bill is an Executive Director of a Christian non-profit that ministers to the needs of men (InfluencersWest.org). He is passionate about God's ability and desire to use men to transform the Kingdom of God here on earth. He loves God and he loves His men, desiring to see them impact their families, work-places, and cities with the love of Jesus Christ. He has become a man of prayer and fervently prays for the men in the ministry and for their wives.

When given the opportunity, he teaches God's word with conviction. His life and the way he practices it has been forever changed. In fact, Bill is so passionate about God's calling on his life, and he is so committed to following Jesus in this ministry, that I was shocked when I learned he still had a career outside of the ministry. He reminds me of a modern day Paul.

God called these two men into a life of ministry and they gladly said yes to Him. The sacrifices they made to pursue Jesus are evident. God may not be calling you to a full-time position as a pastor, but how we live our lives still matters. The people in your world are watching you and are determining whether or not you are a true follower of Christ. Every decision we make, whether it be a big decision or small, is surrendered over to Christ and should reflect a life that is marked by His character. Because we now have the Holy Spirit leading us and guiding us, He will speak to us and help us make the right decisions. Some decisions, like changing the way you do business or making a huge lifestyle change, may be difficult, but necessary. Other changes will not be so dramatic. Either way, as you surrender your life to Christ and choose to follow after Him, you will learn to truly live. If you hang out with Jesus long enough, you will be changed. Follow after Christ and the changes in your life will bring peace, grace, and a purpose.

9

Principle of Purpose

When you follow Christ, you have a change in purpose.

"Now as Jesus was walking by the Sea of Galilee, He saw two brothers, Simon who was called Peter, and Andrew his brother, casting a net into the sea; for they were fishermen. And He said to them, "Follow Me, and I will make you fishers of men."

– Matthew 4:18-19

"I have been crucified with Christ; and it is no longer I who live, but Christ lives in me; and the life which I now live in the flesh I live by faith

*in the Son of God, who loved me and gave
Himself up for me."*

– Galatians 2:20

We are born sinners. No one can truly deny this because we all know the deepest parts of ourselves, our thoughts, and our hidden struggles. If you are still not convinced, just watch little children as they learn to talk. The first words out of their mouths are "me", "mine", and "no". We are all born selfish and rebellious.

As natural born sinners we have one goal and one purpose in life: to please ourselves. We please ourselves by doing everything humanly possible to make this life easier and more enjoyable. We seek to accumulate things like money, homes, and retirement accounts because we believe those things will provide comfort, entertainment, and security. Sometimes we even believe that the people we surround ourselves with and the life we build for ourselves will provide us with a deep abiding sense of love, acceptance, and joy. From birth, we seek to minimize our hurt and discomfort, and to insulate ourselves from pain. We carry these ideals with us all throughout our lives and we find purpose in our achievements and our ability to carry out these ideals.

The truth is we are all living for a purpose, even if we haven't discovered what that purpose is. Whether it is discovered or not, there is something that drives us to do what we do. Some call it drive or passion. I call it purpose.

Have you taken time to analyze where you find your purpose? Is it in making sure you are a good parent, or the best parent when compared to your peers? Is your purpose to be the best son or daughter so that you please your parents no matter what? Is your purpose to be the best friend you can be, always supporting others in their times of need? Or is your purpose to be the best worker so that you can succeed at your career, climb the corporate ladder, and become the expert in your line of work so that others will take notice? Or perhaps you are already the boss and your purpose has become to be the best business owner and employer, working diligently to make sure the business is a success and that your workers admire you. Perhaps you're the student, or an athlete, or a teacher and your purpose has become to excel in those areas. If you are single, you might have a purpose of finding the right spouse so you can start the perfect family. Or is your purpose in making sure you get the right job, so you can have the right income, live in the right neighborhood, drive the right car, and have the perfect children who attend the right school, who get the right grades, friends, and the right "stuff" to make them successful? Or is your purpose found in making sure that other people are happy when they are with you to the point that you have no boundaries and true deep relationships? Or is your purpose to earn lots of money so that you can retire and "enjoy life" before you are too old? Perhaps you find purpose in being the person who knows more about anything and everything so you can truly say you are the smartest person in the group. Finally, you could be the one that finds purpose in proving someone else wrong. You know the feeling, the one you get when someone tells you that you are wrong or can't do something, so you set out to prove that person wrong by succeeding at the very thing that they said was impossible. Many adults are still trying to prove something to their disapproving parents or even after their parents have passed away.

We all use our time, treasures, and talents in fulfilling that which we deem is most important. If something is not that important to you, you simply don't make time for it in your life.

How would an outside observer describe your life? What would a complete stranger say if he came and stayed with you at your home for a month? What would he see, hear, and do with you on a daily and weekly basis?

One time, I was lamenting to a friend that I don't have the time to learn Spanish. As a Zapata, which is a Hispanic surname (perhaps one of the most famous in Mexico), I've always wanted to know how to speak Spanish and even felt that I should *know* Spanish because of my heritage. What my friend said to me hit me square between the eyes and I've never forgotten her response. She said, "If you really felt that strongly about it, you'd find the time." She is right. I have wanted to learn Spanish for a long time, and I think it would be helpful for me in my career, but I have never taken the time to sign up for a course, hire a tutor, or do any of the necessary things required to learn the language. Obviously, what I think in my head, and what I do in my life are two different things. So the question is, "Is learning Spanish that much of a priority for me?" They say actions speak louder than words, so clearly my answer is "no". Learning Spanish is an ideal, but not a priority, and therefore not a purpose I am living for.

We have been given God's Word as a gift and we are to read it, study it, and meditate on it. For centuries people didn't have access to the Bible and it was only available to the religious elite and upper-class in societies. Now, the Bible is the number one selling book in America, yet I would venture to say the least read. We have access to God's word in books, on the Internet, iPads and other tablets, and our smartphones, yet we don't take time to read it. Never before in human history has it been easier to access the Bible and study tools. Sadly, however, we just don't make it a priority because we simply do not purpose in our hearts to know our Creator more.

A colleague of mine once told me he did not have enough time to read the Bible. So I asked him if he had time to read anything else during the day. Proudly he reported that he read multiple newspapers and numerous articles online. Clearly, the issue was not about how much time he had to read, but what he chose to read in the time that he had been given.

There was a period of time when I attended a monthly networking event once a month. At these meetings, I had to park in a parking garage at a hospital. Every time I'd leave, I'd see the same female attendant sitting in her booth reading to pass the time. Her book of choice is the Bible. I saw it EVERY time. Over the months I asked her how she is doing and have found out that her son was going through a divorce and that she was praying for him. I told her that I would pray for her son too and continued to get progress reports when I left the parking garage. So for two minutes each month, I had the privilege of being a source of encouragement to her. More importantly, her testimony and faithfulness to reading the Bible was an encouragement to me in return.

Not all of us can read the Bible while working, but many of us can and I know all of us can make the time, whether it be in the morning, evening, during the commute, or at other times during the day.

My mother-in-law knew a house cleaner who devised a way to distinguish between those who read their Bible and those who did not. She worked for a lot of Christian families who had Bibles in their homes. On a weekly basis, while cleaning, she would move the Bibles from one location to another in the home. Upon her return the next week, she would be able to tell which families had moved the Bible (hopefully to read it), and those that had not. What would happen if she was cleaning your home?

Matthew records the lives of those who were changed by Jesus. He shows how simple fishermen became fishers of men. He shows John the Baptist living with the purpose of proclaiming someone else's authority and not his own. He shows that Jesus Himself lived for a purpose much greater than Himself. Jesus' teachings were so contrary to the beliefs and the culture of His day and they are different than our culture today. Jesus gave His own life that it would become

12 PRINCIPLES OF FOLLOW ME

possible for mankind to be reconciled directly to God the Father by paying the price for our sins.

What is your purpose?

As a parent of two growing boys, I am amazed at the sheer number of things my wife and I need to do to just keep them up to date on their school work. With work, time spent in serving ministries, and their homework, every day is filled with things that need to get done. They are also in midweek kids' programs that require scripture memorization. Between school, church on Sunday, and the mid-week commitments, we are busy. On average, our kids do one sport at a time and usually no more than two different sports a year. During those times we get even busier.

I've seen a trend over the last 20 years when it comes to kids' sports. I don't know if I'm aware because my kids and family are getting older or if things have really changed. I see parents who have their kids in so many sports and other activities that they don't have any time to rest, relax, or focus on the family unit or God. Their lives are consumed with practices, games, rehearsals, and the weekly schedule is a juggling act worthy of a short film documentary. Any observer would be impressed with the mom and dad's ability to have three kids on three different sports teams with three different schedules and never miss a practice or a game. It's not uncommon for some parents to be out three to five nights a week at practices, chauffeuring kids back and forth, grabbing a quick bite to eat on the road, followed up by Saturday and Sunday games, pictures, award ceremonies, and celebrations. It's exhausting just thinking about it. So I must ask, what is the purpose in all this?

Matthew faced similar challenges. What did he want to do with his life? What should he do for a living? How would he survive? Matthew must have asked himself numerous times, "Is being a tax collector worth it?"

He is introduced to us as a wealthy tax collector with many friends. When Jesus dined with him, Jesus was accused by the religious leaders of hanging out with tax collectors and sinners. Clearly, Matthew's purpose in life was different from the leaders and the cultural expectations of his time. He spent his days collecting taxes from his own people. As previously discussed, he was not liked by his own people and was willing to face their criticism and rejection as a tax collector.

One day, Jesus came to him and said, "Follow Me". Immediately Matthew followed Him. One thing is for certain, Matthew saw something in Jesus that he was lacking in himself. Matthew was educated, wealthy, in a position of power, protected by the Romans, and admired by many and despised by even more. What benefits would he gain by giving it all up to follow Jesus? What was missing?

After choosing to follow Jesus, Matthew found his true purpose. He left all that he had accumulated behind and followed after Jesus. His purpose went from being a tax collector for the Roman Empire, to being a soul gatherer for the Kingdom of God. What had been lacking in his life before Christ was now filled.

Matthew penned these words, which he learned from His Savior, "But seek first His kingdom and His righteousness; and all these things shall be added to you" (Matthew 6:33). Clearly this is a departure from his pre-Jesus encounter.

Matthew is also the disciple that directed his Gospel (the Book of Matthew) toward the Jews. As a Jew himself, he knew what all Jews were looking for in their Messiah. They knew the prophecies that would need to be fulfilled by the Messiah as proof. And more than any of the other writers of the Gospel, he references the Old Testament prophecies and shows how Jesus fulfilled them. He knew what to look for in the Messiah and he knew that the promise God made to Abraham, the father of the Jews, was being fulfilled. Through the person and life of Jesus Christ, God's promise to

Abraham, that he and his descendents would be a blessing to all mankind, was actually happening! Perhaps that is why Matthew ended his book with a call to all Christians to go out and make disciples of all men, baptizing them in the name of the Father, Son, and Holy Spirit.

Matthew's own purpose went from being a tax collector to becoming a follower of Jesus Christ, then to being an evangelist and author for Christ. Eventually he was martyred for his faith. His life's purpose changed and the world changed because of it.

It's interesting to note that none of the writers in the New Testament encouraged Christians to take on politics as their purpose. I know it's not popular to mix politics and religion, but in our country there are many Christians who have made it their sole purpose in life to influence what happens politically. Early Christians weren't encouraged to challenge the laws, overthrow the government, or to fight for their rights. Instead, they were taught allegiance to God's Kingdom and to proclaim His Gospel no matter the cost. They understood that God uses the leaders of nations and governments to bring out His plan on the earth. As Christians, we are commanded to respect our leaders, obey authority, pray for them, and to abide by the laws that do not contradict the Bible. We are to work toward proclaiming

Christ to all mankind that all might come to know Him personally, regardless of what the government does or does not do. I'm not saying that we should abstain from taking an active role in shaping the future of our country by voting, debating, and being informed. I'm saying that this should not be our purpose. Our purpose is to love Christ and to follow Him and lead others to Him.

Matthew had to make sacrifices and faced persecution from his family, friends, and leaders in order to live out his commitment to follow Christ. Church history records that he eventually died as a martyr for Christ.

In your heart, you know what your purpose is and what you are living for. What will the rest of your life reveal to others about your purpose?

If you know you need to re-order your life, there are many resources and tools available to anyone who wants to better understand how to discover their God-given purpose. Rick Warren states in his book, *The Purpose Driven Life*, that it starts with realizing that life is not about you. God has a purpose and a plan for your life and He has made you in such a way to fulfill that purpose.[5]

If you are wealthy, invest it in God's Kingdom. If you lose everything in this life, the investments you made in winning souls for Jesus when you had money, will be the only investment that mattered. Money does not give you worth or purpose. It's entrusted to you by God to re-invest into long-term eternal stocks and securities by using it for Him to bring the knowledge of Jesus Christ to a lost world. Can you win souls with money? No, not directly, but you can invest in ministries and resources that will use money to proclaim the Gospel to people who have not heard it.

As Christ followers, we have the Holy Spirit inside of us speaking to us, giving us direction, and calling us to follow Him. Every believer is called to spread the news of Jesus Christ to our family, friends, and neighbors. We don't need to "discover" this truth and purpose because we are commanded to do it.

There has never been a better time for you and your family to surrender everything to Christ and ask Him how you should plan your days, weeks, and years. Make it a priority to block out time for God-centered activities. Spend time in prayer and quiet reflection in the Bible, seeking His counsel and presence.

One Christmas, our family decided to donate all of our Christmas budget to ministries rather than getting gifts for ourselves. My wife and I, and our two boys, both under 10 at the time, did not receive any gifts for Christmas. We notified all our family members and friends that we were not "doing" Christmas and that if they wished to give our family gifts that we would prefer them to give the money away. For those that did send us money, we turned around and gave it all away. The observation I made a few days after Christmas was that our family, especially our children, were not scarred for life because they didn't get gifts. It didn't traumatize them and leave them depressed and sad. In fact, on Christmas day we had extra time and we decided to visit a local Assisted Living Facility where we delivered homemade ornaments to the residents who were there. Many of the people would not have received any visitors had we not come, and it was our way of saying "God loves you" to those who desperately need it. We will always remember the year we didn't "do" Christmas, because what we received in return were memories that will last a lifetime instead of toys that would be old, outdated, broken, and replaced within a year.

Nearly every church has a list of opportunities to serve their community in various ways. Whether it be helping feed the homeless, doing maintenance on the home of an elderly person, cleaning up the streets, visiting shut-ins, praying for the hurting and discouraged, teaching Sunday School to elementary, Junior High, and High School children. Take the opportunity to invest in God's kingdom.

Find your purpose in something other than yourself. Ask God to direct you in the right direction and then take the steps necessary to fulfill His purpose for the life He has given you.

10

Principle of Preparation

A follower of Christ is prepared to live for Christ, suffer for Him, and be ready for His return.

"As He was sitting on the Mount of Olives, the disciples came to Him privately, saying, 'Tell us, when will these things happen, and what will be the sign of Your coming, and of the end of the age?'

And Jesus answered and said to them, 'See to it that no one misleads you. For many will come in My name, saying, "I am the Christ," and will mislead many. You will be hearing of wars and rumors of wars. See that you are not frightened, for those things must take place, but that is not yet the end. For nation will rise against nation, and kingdom against kingdom, and in various places there will be famines and earthquakes. But all these things are merely the beginning of birth pangs. Then they will deliver you to tribulation, and will kill you, and you will be hated by all nations because of My name. At that time many will fall away and will betray one another and hate one another. Many false prophets will arise and will mislead many. Because lawlessness is increased, most people's love will grow cold. But the one who endures to the end, he will be saved. This gospel of the kingdom shall be preached in the whole world as a testimony to all the nations, and then the end will come."

– Matthew 24:3-14

As a Jewish boy, Matthew would have been raised in a home that celebrated Passover every year. The dinner was a ceremonious occasion filled with symbolism and rituals that served to remind the Jews of their long and arduous history where God delivered them from the bondage and slavery in Egypt. Not only were they reminded of their past, they were also reminded that they were looking for Elijah to return to prepare the way for the Messiah. They longed for their Deliverer.

Unlike most of his contemporaries, Matthew accepted the call to follow Jesus. He was prepared for the Messiah and when Jesus asked him to follow Him, he responded "yes". He did not put off the decision, but immediately followed. Not only was he prepared to follow, he was also prepared to suffer.

As a disciple of Christ, he spent time living with Him, watched Him, ate with Him, learned from Him, and continued as an Apostle after Christ ascended into heaven. According to tradition, Matthew was killed as a martyr by the king of Ethiopia after rebuking him for lusting after his own niece [6]. Even until death, he lived for Christ.

Matthew knew that standing for truth and for Christ would eventually lead to suffering. He saw Jesus arrested, falsely accused, beaten and tortured, and crucified on the cross. He writes with intensity and passion knowing that many will not be prepared. You can sense this by his stories, choice of words and the inclusion of the sufferings of Christ in his Gospel. He wants Christ's followers to be prepared for the suffering that will come as they chose to live for Christ and to be prepared for Christ's return.

These warnings from Jesus are clearly stated, "And brother will deliver up brother to death, and a father his child; and children will rise up against parents, and cause them to be put to death. And you will be hated by all on account of My name, but it is the one who has endured to the end who will be saved" (Matthew 10:21-22). In other words, there is no way around it, His followers will be rejected simply because they follow Him.

Jesus taught His disciples how to handle rejection by how He endured suffering. He wanted us to be ready for suffering because it will come.

No one wants to suffer. Let's face it, when given the option of pain or pleasure, normal people will choose pleasure every time. Suffering for your opinions and beliefs is hard because it hurts emotionally and spiritually, and sometimes physically. In the American culture, for the most part, Christians have to endure ridicule, isolation, rejection, and side-lining. Rarely are we physically harmed. We really do have it easy.

In other countries, choosing to be a Christian is a choice to die. A 2013 article published by Fox News citing the Vatican stated that over 100,000 Christians are killed annually and that the persecution against Christians is on the rise worldwide.[7]

Jesus said we would be hated on account of Him and nothing tests the commitment of a follower of Christ like suffering does. When your family, co-workers, and neighbors turn on you and your job is at risk or your physical safety is at stake, your faith is tested. The question we need to ask ourselves is, "*Am I ready for that?*" I need to be. We must all be ready and willing to suffer for Him. The best news is that one day we will be with Jesus in heaven and all suffering will be gone.

We are encouraged to look ahead to that day and Matthew wants us to be ready for when Christ returns. With meticulous detail he recorded the prophecies which Jesus fulfilled as a way to prove to the Jews and the world that Jesus was the Messiah.

Just as Matthew didn't want his family, friends, or anyone he knew to miss Jesus (especially his fellow Jews), he doesn't want any of us to miss out on knowing the Messiah either. He knew firsthand that many people simply ignored Jesus or chose not to believe in Him for various reasons. Matthew also knew that one day Jesus is going to return and he wants us to be ready.

If Jesus were to come back today would you be ready?

In Matthew 24 Jesus says that we do not know the day that He is coming back and that it will happen at an hour when we do not think it will. It will be quick, sudden, and unpredictable like a lightning flash. Not even the angels in heaven know when Christ will return. Even though we don't know the exact time of His return we are told that it will be like in the days of Noah when the great Flood came upon the earth. What were the days of Noah like?

For over 100 years Noah built a huge boat. While he was building the ark he warned the people that God was going to destroy the world. How did the people respond? They thought he was crazy and no one listened. It says in Matthew 24:38 that before the flood came they were eating and drinking, marrying and being given in marriage, until the day that Noah entered into the ark. The passage goes on to tell us that they did not understand what was happening until the day they were destroyed. In Genesis 6:5 it says, "The LORD saw that the wickedness of man was great on the earth, and that every intent of the thoughts of his heart was only evil continually."

Our world is looking more and more like that today. Events are happening that resemble the warning signs given to us by God Himself that signal that His return is near. World events like wars, natural disasters, and other "birth pangs" are upon us and we are not alert. We are not watching. We are too busy with life and living to stop and observe and see what is happening around us.

We react to the news of Jesus like we react to the flight attendants as they go through their pre-boarding safety routine for the passengers. As they stand in the aisle demonstrating how the seatbelts, oxygen masks, seat cushions, lighting and doors operate in an emergency situation, most people tune out. The attendants don't stand there and do the routine every flight for their own benefit. They know how everything works and they are ready for the unexpected. The passengers, on the other hand, either take the "*Yeah, yeah...I know this stuff already*" approach, or are too busy to pay attention. They've put in their earphones, are reading, busy checking last minute emails and text messages on their phones, or are already trying to fall asleep. Being truly prepared for an emergency is not on their priority list because they don't think they will need it.

While it is true that most may never need to use the flotation devices located under the seats or the mysterious oxygen masks most people have never seen, everyone will have to face Jesus one day and will be held accountable for their lives. Jesus is coming back and most will not be ready for it. It says in Matthew 24:42, "Therefore be on the alert, for you do not know which day your Lord is coming." In other words, pay attention and be ready!

When will Christ return? No one knows. But a follower of Christ must be prepared. Even if Jesus does not come in your lifetime, your life on earth is not guaranteed to be long. No one is promised tomorrow. If we are not promised tomorrow, we must be ready to meet our Maker today.

We all know those who have died suddenly without warning or reason including the friend who passes away in their sleep in their 30's, the father who dies of cancer when he is 40 and leaves behind four children and a wife, the 18 year old daughter or son who never wakes up or dies in an accident, and the list goes on. Life is short and when it's over, it's over. There are no second chances.

The Book of Hebrews teaches that each of us has an appointed time to die and when that happens, we will be judged. We will stand before God and have to give account for the life that we lived here on earth (Hebrews 9:27).

For those who were ready and who chose to follow Christ, that day will be a day of rejoicing because they will see their Savior face-to-face. They will know first-hand true forgiveness and eternal love. For those that are not prepared for that day, they will face judgment and condemnation. They will be cast away from the presence of the Almighty God of love and sent to hell.

God is a God of love and justice. He says that mercy triumphs over judgment, yet He made it very clear in scripture that eternal life cannot be found apart from a true relationship with Jesus (John 14:6). If you do not choose Jesus while you are alive, you will not get to choose Him after death.

In the movie *The Secrets of Jonathan Sperry* there is a scene where Jonathan Sperry, an older gentleman in a small town who decided to disciple a handful of Junior High boys, takes them to a graveyard. He asks them to listen to the gravestones. With a raspy quiet voice he cries out, "Why? Why? Why didn't you tell me about Jesus?" He's teaching the boys that they only have one chance to share the gospel with others in this world. That chance is while we are alive.[8]

The scene is a vivid picture of the reality we all face. Are we too afraid to tell people about God's love, the provision of a Savior, and our need of salvation? Are we letting people pass into eternity without doing our part to prepare them for what is to come? What can we do about it?

Be prepared. Don't put off the decision to follow Christ until tomorrow. Be ready. Watch for His coming and live your life as though it were your last day on earth. Who do you love that does not know Jesus? Who do you work with that is living in spiritual blindness and needs to see? Decide today that you can no longer put off telling them that they can repent and have their sins forgiven by our loving Heavenly Father who eagerly awaits for them. Reconcile today. Repent today. Prepare today.

11

Principle of Prayer

A follower of Christ prays.

> *Jesus said, "Pray, then, in this way: 'Our Father who is in heaven, Hallowed be Your name. Your kingdom come. Your will be done, on earth as it is in heaven.*
>
> *Give us this day our daily bread. And forgive us our debts, as we also have forgiven our debtors.*
>
> *And do not lead us into temptation, but deliver us from evil. For Yours is the kingdom and the power and the glory forever. Amen.'*
>
> *For if you forgive others for their transgressions, your heavenly Father will also forgive you.*
>
> *– Matthew 6:9-14*

Prayer, in its simplest terms, is having a conversation with God. Immediately after Jesus died on the cross there was an earthquake and the veil hanging in the Temple that separated the innermost part of the Sanctuary from the outside was torn in two. The symbolism is unmistakable; the need for a mediator between God the Father and mankind came to an end. The role of the Priest as the go-between of God and man as required by the Laws of the Old Testament was fulfilled in Christ.

You see, in the Old Testament, God appointed the men from the family tribe of Levi as priests to maintain the Temple and offer all the sacrifices for the sins of the people. The people would bring their offerings and their sacrifices to the Levites who would then turn and offer them to God on behalf of that person. Anyone who was not specifically set apart to perform work on or near the Temple was not allowed near the holiest part of the Temple.

God established the system that required there to be a go-between. The books of Leviticus and Numbers give us detailed accounts of the requirements that God placed on His people.

The amazing thing about Christ's death is the fact that God's own requirement for the intermediary was fulfilled in Christ Himself. We now have direct access to God the Father through Jesus Christ living in us. The same God that created the separation between Him and mankind now bridged the gap with His Son, Jesus.

So when you see the first disciples ask Jesus to teach them how to pray, it makes sense because they were not accustom to praying the way they saw Jesus praying. The priests were primarily responsible for offering sacrifices and communicating with God on behalf of the people. I'm sure this is one reason Matthew recorded instructions from Jesus, the perfect High Priest, on how to talk to the Father. Praying directly to the Father and experiencing power through prayer was new to them.

Matthew highlights the fact that Jesus was a praying man. If we are to follow Him, we too, are to be praying men and women.

So how do we pray?

Jesus was very clear both in His instructions and in His practice of prayer. Essentially, we see Him praying all the time. He is in a constant dialogue with His Father about everything.

When He healed a person, He prayed. When He finished a really tough day, He withdrew to pray. When He was facing tough decisions, He prayed. When He ate, He prayed. When He grieved, He prayed.

The most dramatic prayer event of Christ's life was just before He was betrayed by one of His own disciples, arrested, and subsequently killed. In Matthew 26 we see that He spent hours passionately pleading with God, His Father, in prayer. While doing so, He encouraged His followers to pray.

There's no secret formula to what prayer looks like. There's no special feeling that must be felt in order to know that you are doing it right. And, there is no guarantee that everything you pray for will turn out the way you have asked for it to.

I saw a video by Louie Giglio that put this into perspective for me. He compared the world to a golf ball. If the world were a golf ball, the sun would be a ball 15 feet in diameter and the largest star we know to exist would be the size of the Golden Gate Bridge in San Francisco. He gave those illustrations to show that our God is HUGE![9] He is infinite and we can go to Him with our greatest concerns and our greatest trials and with our greatest praise. God is not to be viewed simply as your "servant in the sky". Instead, we are to humbly come before Him in prayer as the wonderful Creator of all things.

An acronym I learned when I was young that has helped me to remember what to pray for and how to pray, uses the word **P.R.A.Y.**

P - Praise

R - Repent

A - Ask

Y - Yield

P - **Praise**. If you look at the Lord's Prayer you will see that it starts with praising God. That's a great way to start off your prayer because it helps focus on who God is.

In Habakkuk 3:16-19 we are given a wonderful example of what to do when it seems as though the world is crashing in. It says:

"I heard and my inward parts trembled, at the sound my lips quivered. Decay enters my bones, and in my place I tremble.

Because I must wait quietly for the day of distress, for the people to arise who will invade us.

Though the fig tree should not blossom and there be no fruit on the vines, though the yield of the olive should fail and the fields produce no food, though the flock should be cut off from the fold and there be no cattle in the stalls, **yet I will**

exult (rejoice in NIV) in the Lord, I will
rejoice in the God of my salvation.

The Lord God is my strength, and He has made
my feet like hinds' feet, and makes me walk on
my high places." (emphasis added)

When you feel totally helpless, hopeless, and bound for disaster, we are told to praise the God of our Salvation. Praise is usually the last thing to go when the going gets tough, but it's the first thing Jesus taught us to do when we come to our Father.

There have been many times in my life when praising God was the last thing I wanted to do. It's not easy to praise God when dealing with grief, anger, loss, disappointment, pain, and all the other negative emotions we experience. But praise changes our perspective on things when we are at the lowest points. I can't explain it, but it does make things better.

R - Repent. When coming to God, it's important that we repent. In fact, the idea of coming into the presence of a holy God and not being aware of my sin seems ridiculous. When I look at how I pray, however, I realize that I do just that...I burst into asking for things without praising or repenting.

Isaiah was shown how sinful he was when God gave him a peek into heaven where God was seated on the throne, lofty and exalted. Angels flew about Him covering their face and feet exclaiming, "Holy, Holy, Holy, is the LORD of hosts, the whole earth is full of His glory." Immediately seeing this and hearing it, Isaiah's first response was to declare his own sinfulness and the sinfulness of his people (Isaiah 6:1-5). How could I, a sinner, approach a holy God, without being aware of my sin? Honestly, I don't fully understand how I do that, but I still do. Despite all my sin, God still listens to me. I know He does this because He Himself said that if we confess our sin He is gracious to forgive us of all sin and cleanses us from unrighteousness (1 John 1:9).

David wrote that when he concealed his sin, his body wasted away and that his energy was drained as with the fever heat of summer until he confessed his sins to God (Psalm 32:3-4). It was eating him from the inside out. When we confess our sin, we bring it before God and He forgives us.

A - Ask. Jesus Himself taught us to ask for our daily bread. He also taught us not to worry about tomorrow. It's okay to ask for God to do things and to work on your behalf. David, the King of Israel, pleaded with God to direct and protect him over and over again. Jesus taught us to ask, seek, and knock.

*"Ask, and it will be given to you; seek, and you
will find; knock, and it will be opened to you.
For everyone who asks receives, and he who seeks
finds, and to him who knocks it will be opened."*

– Matthew 7:7-8

Remember to pray for others too. Bringing the needs of others to your heavenly Father will help take your eyes off of your own life as you intercede for others.

Paul encourages us to pray for all things all the time (1Thessalonians 5:17). In Luke we read of a parable where Jesus encourages us to pray like a widow who is continually seeking protection from a king. Eventually the king grants the request because the widow is relentless in her pleas (Luke 18). We are to always go to Jesus with our requests.

Y - Yield. Stop, reflect, and listen for God to respond. Too many times we forget to yield as we just plow ahead in our prayers. Prayer is a two-way conversation, just like talking with a friend. You'd never expect to have a great friendship with someone if all they did was come to you and ask, ask, ask, or talk non-stop and then never give you a chance to respond to talk yourself.

By yielding, we give God a chance to work in our heart and to teach us as we position ourselves in a place of humility, acknowledging that God will always do what is in our best interest. Immediately following the "ask, and it will be given" lesson by Jesus recorded in Matthew 7:7-8, Jesus goes on to compare our heavenly Father to human fathers. He says, "Or what man is there among you who, when his son asks for a loaf, will give him a stone? Or if he asks for a fish, he will not give him a snake, will he? If you then, being evil, know how to give good gifts to your children, how much more will your Father who is in heaven give what is good to those who ask Him!" (Matthew 7:9-11). In other words, we have a really awesome Father who hears us and gives us what we need because He loves us with a perfect love. He is not mean, vindictive, or *I'm-going-to-make-you-feel-guilty*, kind of dad. When we yield we can rest, knowing that He's got everything under control.

How do you start praying? You just do it. Right now, you can stop reading and turn your heart and your attention to God and start a conversation. It starts with a single word and goes from there. If you don't know what to pray, open the Bible to any book in the New Testament, and with a prayerful attitude read it back to God, asking Him to speak to you through His Word.

Don't be afraid to talk to the One who already knows your thoughts and who loves you. That's right, God made you and has been in love with you since before you were created. He is excited about you and wants to talk with you all the time from the moment you wake up to when you go to bed and every moment in between. Now that you know that He *wants* to talk to you, and that He probably *has* been talking to you, start listening and then start talking back. Prayer is simply an ongoing conversation between you and your heavenly Father. In fact, it shouldn't ever stop.

Talk to Him about everything and anything. Nothing is too big, and nothing is too small. Nothing will be a surprise to Him either because He already knows everything.

Many Christ followers reluctantly say "all I can do is pray" when they hear about a need and aren't able to do anything else. The truth of the matter is that prayer should never be a last resort measure. Prayer is to be the first thing, the first response in every circumstance. Prayer is the best and most powerful weapon in our arsenal to fight against the darkness in this world.

I recently met an old friend during a work project. We hadn't seen each other in a few years and while we were catching up on what was happening with our families he shared with me that he and his wife were going through a tough time trying to decide which church to attend. It had come to the point where it was creating friction in their marriage because they held different opinions. We talked about it for a while and then I felt led to pray for my friend. Rather than telling him that I would pray for him, I asked him right there if I could pray for him. He encouraged me to continue, so in the middle of the parking lot, we prayed.

The next day he called me to thank me for praying for him. Sadly, I wouldn't be surprised if I was the first person to pray with him in person about this matter. Not only was God glorified in the moment, but we came together asking Him for a solution and my friend was impacted by the prayer. Prayer is powerful.

Devote specific time where you will stop what you are doing and pray. Make it a point to always pray throughout all your daily activities. Invite God to be a part of everything you do and to speak to you. Ask Him to make you attentive to His voice so that, just like the disciples, He can teach you how to pray.

A follower of Christ prays.

12

Principle of a Changed Person

A follower of Christ becomes a new person in Christ.

"If any man is in Christ, he is a new creation.
The old has gone, behold new things have come."

— 2 Corinthians 5:17

"Let your light shine before men in such a way
that they may see your good works, and glorify
your Father who is in heaven."

— Matthew 5:16

"But I say to you, love your enemies and pray for
those who persecute you so that you may be sons
of your Father who is in heaven."

— Matthew 5:44

When you look at all the changes that took place in Matthew's life, you realize that ultimately he was a changed person in every way from the inside and out. Even his name was changed from Levi to Matthew. The word Matthew means "a gift from God". Can you imagine? He went from being Levi, the dejected and hated tax collector, to becoming a gift from God. What an amazing transformation.

When a person becomes a follower of Christ, he becomes a new creation. Jesus called it "born again", and it's like coming alive for the second time. This time it's a spiritual life.

Imagine, if you will, that we are all like caterpillars eagerly waiting to become butterflies. The transformation of a caterpillar into a butterfly is nothing short of a miracle and the change is impossible to miss. When we choose to follow Christ we go through a spiritual transformation just as dramatic and miraculous.

For some, the change is colossal and happens overnight. There are those that are immediately delivered from drug and other addictions and never go back. For others, the changes are more subtle and develop over time as their relationship with Christ grows.

The theological term for this transformation is sanctification. It's the process of changing to become more like Christ in how we think, act, and live life. The old self, along with its habits, has to be laid aside never to be taken up again by the power of the Holy Spirit as He empowers us to live in holiness.

When a person makes a genuine choice to follow after Christ completely, he is making a choice to take on this new life. We've already examined 11 principles and how they affect a follower's life, and from them you can see that life is different once you make the decision to follow Christ. Jesus makes it very clear there is no option of returning to the life that you once knew. The old life, with all of its false promises, corruptions, and darkness, is no longer desired. This new surrendered life is filled with meaning, satisfaction, and direction.

It's important to note that once you have decided to follow Christ it doesn't result in a life that is absent of all trials. In fact, it's quite the opposite.

As I noted previously, Matthew records Jesus' story of two different men. One is a fool, and the other is wise. Both men face rain, floods, and winds, but the man who built his house upon the rock was able to weather the storm. He was able to endure the trials of life. The one who built his house on the sand lost everything. The difference between the two homes was the foundation on which they were built. The wise man was considered wise because he heard the words of Jesus and acted on them. The fool heard the same words but failed to take action (Matthew 7:24-27). Becoming a Christian does not exempt you from trials and troubles. Placing your hope in Christ and obeying Him creates the opportunity for you to weather the trial instead of being destroyed.

The Apostle Paul also warns Timothy, a young pastor, of this truth when he tells him that all who desire to live a life of godliness will be persecuted and face trials (2 Timothy 3:12).

Before Paul penned those words, Jesus said this world would reject His followers just like they rejected Him. He warned His disciples over and over that they would face tough trials and hardships that would test their commitment to Him. In Matthew 4:9 He states, "Then they will deliver you to tribulation, and will kill you, and you will be hated by all nations because of My name." When you pause to think about it, it makes sense. This world has sold us a false bill of goods. The world promises happiness and pleasure in money, sex, security, drugs, alcohol, music, video games and other forms of entertainment and hundreds of other ways. Everything this world offers, however, falls short of complete satisfaction.

When a person decides to follow Christ their opinion of the world changes. A different opinion means a different lifestyle, and when you choose not to participate in the ways of the world because you now know the truth (that these activities cannot satisfy), you will be rejected by others. Your friends, family, and even your own children may reject you as you follow Christ. Rejection is not easy, but it's going to happen somewhere, somehow.

Even among other "Christians" there is a strong possibility that you will be rejected as you live out the life that Jesus called you to because not everyone who calls him or herself "Christian" is really a follower of Christ. Jesus Himself said, "Every good tree bears good fruit, but the bad tree bears bad fruit. A good tree cannot produce bad fruit, nor can a bad tree produce good fruit. Every tree that does not bear good fruit is cut down and thrown into the fire. So then, you will know them by their fruits" (Matthew 7:17-20). In other words, true Christ followers experience life transformation. Those that do not know Him remain unchanged.

The following verse is further evidence that those who claim to follow Christ but don't have a changed life are not going to be with Jesus in eternity. Jesus said, "Not everyone who says to Me, 'Lord, Lord,' will enter the kingdom of heaven, but he who does the will of My Father who is in heaven will enter" (Matthew 7:21).

Doing the will of my Father is another way of saying that our lives have been changed. We were once enemies of God with rebellion ingrained in our hearts and minds, but now we are friends with Him, seeking to know Him and His will while obeying His commands.

There are many people in the Bible who went through this radical transformation. In many cases, but not all, God gave them new names to signify this change.

Abram became Abraham as he followed God's calling to leave his home and go to a land unknown to him. Abraham's wife became Sarah and was no longer called Sarai. Jacob, which means "heel-catcher" because he was holding on the heel of his twin brother at birth, became Israel, which means to persevere with God. Joseph was sold into slavery by his brothers but became a powerful leader in Egypt because his focus was on God's plan, not his. He could have been bitter and sought revenge upon them; instead he saw God's hand in it and was a changed man. David was a lowly shepherd boy that became Israel's most beloved king. Mary, a young single girl, engaged to be married, faced the shame and condemnation that being pregnant brought, when she submitted to God's will to carry the Messiah in her womb. Cephas became Peter after following Christ. Christ gave him the name "the rock" as a representation of the role that he would play in the Church despite his well noted failures. Saul, a hater and persecutor of Christians, became Paul, the world's greatest missionary ever known. And Levi, the hated tax collector, became Matthew, the beloved one.

True and genuine faith in Jesus results in a changed life that expresses itself through action and the way we live. I am a changed person because I follow Jesus. My wife is a changed woman because she chooses to follow Christ. Our children, when they accepted Christ, were changed. As parents, we could see it.

Everyone that has a true encounter with Christ and makes the decision to follow Him will be changed.

CONCLUSION

This book took me five years to write and just as many before I published it. Most of my time is dedicated to the multiple businesses I own. My wife and I lead a small group at my church and we have two children. At first, I started writing this book for you, the reader. However, over time I realized that I needed to write this for myself. Never in my life have I kept focus on a thought for so long. For five years these principles were on the forefront of my mind taking shape and being refined. Over the years I've been able to see how these principles are lived out and it has been convicting because at times I don't always find myself doing what I have written in these pages. These principles, however, were not listed as a way to create a checklist of things to do. Instead, I pray that our inability to always do what we know to be the right thing to do, will serve as a reminder to all of us that we are all saved by grace. Our salvation is not the result of works, otherwise we would all boast about how great we are. No, we are saved by our faith in Jesus Christ. And that faith is a life transforming faith.

Our power, position, proximity, priorities, possessions, practices, purpose, prayer, perspective, plans, preparation, and who we are as a person, are all brought before our Lord Jesus Christ when we choose to follow Him. Before following Christ we found value, worth, and security in many of them based on the world's definition. When we choose to follow Christ everything gets placed into His hands and we go where that leads us. The temptation we all face is to revert to our old habits and to forget that these changes are necessary. We "fall away" from Christ and justify why we haven't spent any quality time with Him in the Word and in prayer. We get our priorities mixed up again. We begin to hoard our possessions because we don't truly trust that God will provide if we give everything away. Over time, if we let these things slip, our lives return to the way they once were. When that happens we are destined for disaster.

As I was writing this book I began to realize that it appears as though we must be perfect in order to be followers of Christ. The "Principle of Perfection", however, is not one of the principles found anywhere in the book of Matthew. Some of you, no doubt, are familiar with the verse in Matthew 5:48 where Jesus says, "Be perfect, therefore, as your heavenly Father is perfect" and have been trying to live the perfect life for Jesus, attempting to be perfect in every way. When we think of perfection we tend to think only of the outward actions and how we conduct ourselves. In other words, we consider ourselves perfect if we don't break any of the rules.

After a lengthy discourse by Jesus to his followers regarding human relationships and how we are to live, Jesus lays it on them with that phrase, "be perfect, therefore, as your heavenly Father is perfect." My first thought after reading that was that I needed to strive for perfection and truly be perfect...in every way. And indeed, that is what He said. But this comes right in the middle of his Sermon on the Mount where He is creating a contrast between the popular theology of His day and the way God sees things.

At this point in the sermon, He had just finished explaining how our faith and righteous living needed to exceed that of the scribes and the Pharisees (Matthew 5:20) who, at that time, were considered to be the most righteous people in their day, upholding the strictest of living standards in order to please God. Not only did they attempt to uphold the Law, but they created additional laws and standards to abide by so that, when followed perfectly, you'd avoid the potential of accidentally breaking all of the official Laws.

What Jesus is saying is that their popular belief and system of rule following did not equate to true discipleship or holiness. To prove His point, He set the standard of holiness so high and so impossible that none of them, or any of us for that matter, could achieve it. He is making a concluding point that essentially states that in order to be perfect by God's standard we must be able to uphold every aspect of the Law *AND* every aspect of God's perfection in every area of our lives. No one can do that!

Immediately after demanding perfection Jesus goes on to warn His followers to be careful about practicing their righteousness before men in order to be noticed by them. He warns against making a big scene when giving away money (Matthew 6:1-4). He says to pray privately unlike the hypocrites who would pray publicly to be noticed by others (6:5-15). He gives instructions on how to properly fast (6:16-18) and what to do with wealth (6:19-34) and then goes on to give instructions on judging others and describing true righteous living (Matthew 7).

Tucked in the middle of that discourse, shortly after issuing the declaration that we are to be perfect is the "Lord's Prayer". In that prayer we are taught to pray these words, "And forgive us our debts, as we also have forgiven our debtors. And do not lead us into temptation, but deliver us from evil" (Matthew 6:12-13). He goes on to say that if we forgive others then our Father will forgive us (14-15).

It is clear that Jesus knows it is impossible for us to be perfect and that His statement, if taken out of context, can convey the wrong point. Why else would He teach us how to pray the Lord's Prayer and then emphasize our need to forgive in order to be forgiven?

He knows what we all know to be true. It is impossible to be perfect because we are born sinners. It's because of our imperfection, our sins, that Christ, who was and is perfect, died for us. That is why we need Christ to begin with.

The Apostle Paul, a former Pharisee, knew first-hand the emptiness found in trying to live the perfect life without Jesus. Romans Chapter 7 describes every person's struggle to keep all the rules without the help of Jesus and His Spirit. In other parts of his writings he describes us as imperfect and calls Jesus the perfect one (1 Corinthians 13:10) that is to come. In Hebrews we see that the Law declared everything imperfect (7:19) and that Jesus was the only One made perfect (5:9).

So, lest we forget, and try to make this into a book of do's and don'ts, we must remember that Jesus Himself said He came for the sinners and not the righteous. The principles spelled out here are not going to save you, only a true love for and a faith in Jesus Christ will do that.

God calls us to be holy because He is holy, but we are born sinners, bent toward doing what is wrong. It was in that life (the life of sin), that Christ died for us. He does not need perfect followers, for if that were the case, He would have none. None of us are perfect and all of us need a Savior.

Pastor Pete McKenzie said this in a Bible study and I wanted to share it with you because I believe it truly summarizes what the true follower of Jesus desires:

Do you walk out your door each day saying the following?

> *"Today, I want to be just like Jesus in all my conduct,*
> *in all my encounters,*
> *in all my business dealings,*
> *and in my interactions with my family and neighbors.*
> *I want to drive like Jesus,*
> *talk like Jesus,*

think like Jesus,
shop like Jesus,
eat like Jesus,
dress like Jesus,
help like Jesus,
encourage like Jesus,
take an insult like Jesus,
read what Jesus would read,
spend my time like Jesus would spend His time,
spend my money like Jesus,
love others like Jesus,
treat my enemies like Jesus treated His,
have in my house what Jesus would have in His
house.
I want to be a friend like Jesus,
a lover like Jesus,
have the insight and wisdom of Jesus,
and the courage and lack of fear that He
had."[10]

When I heard him preach this, I was convicted because I know that I fail in many ways. I know that I'm not perfect, yet I do strive to follow Jesus in every aspect of my life and I praise God that not one of us is saved by the works that we do, but by the grace of God. There is nothing we can possibly do well enough to deserve the salvation that has been provided through the perfect work of Jesus when He died on the cross for my sins and for yours.

It is my closing prayer that you will now go and follow Him as I have chosen to follow Him. For we know that if there is hope for Levi, a despised and sinful tax collector, there is hope for all of us.

CONTACT THE AUTHOR

Email:	aaron@aaronzapata.com
Twitter:	@aaronzapata
Instagram:	@aaronzapata
Online:	www.AaronZapata.com

NOTES

[1] *Dictionary.com Unabridged.* Random House, Inc. 17 Oct. 2013. <Dictionary.com http://dictionary.reference.com/browse/Providence>.

[2] Richard Stearns, *The Hole In Our Gospel,* (Nashville: Thomas Nelson, 2009), 27-28.

[3] http://en.wikipedia.org/wiki/Spherical_Earth.

[4] Mark Mittleberg, *Choosing Your Faith...In a World of Spiritual Options,* (Carol Stream, IL: Tyndale), 85-94.

[5] Rick Warren, *The Purpose Driven Life,* (Grand Rapids: Zondervan), 17.

[6] http://en.wikipedia.org/wiki/The_Martyrdom_of_Saint_Matthew_(Caravaggio)

[7] http://www.foxnews.com/world/2013/06/02/vatican-spokesman-claims-100000-christians-killed-annually-because-faith/

[8] *The Secrets of Jonathan Sperry,* Dir. Rich Christiano. Christiano Film Group, 2008. DVD.

[9] "How Great Is Our God: Louie Giglio" Online video clip, accessed 11 November 2013. <http://youtu.be/PtpTk2ENq7o>

[10] Pete McKenzie, Influencers West Bible Study, October 23, 2013

www.ingramcontent.com/pod-product-compliance
Lightning Source LLC
LaVergne TN
LVHW021345080426
835508LV00020B/2121

9 781736 074503